Bedouins

Also from Westphalia Press
westphaliapress.org

The Idea of the Digital University

Dialogue in the Roman-Greco World

The History of Photography

International or Local Ownership?: Security Sector Development in Post-Independent Kosovo

Lankes, His Woodcut Bookplates

Opportunity and Horatio Alger

The Role of Theory in Policy Analysis

The Little Confectioner

Non-Profit Organizations and Disaster

The Idea of Neoliberalism: The Emperor Has Threadbare Contemporary Clothes

Social Satire and the Modern Novel

Ukraine vs. Russia: Revolution, Democracy and War: Selected Articles and Blogs, 2010-2016

James Martineau and Rebuilding Theology

A Strategy for Implementing the Reconciliation Process

Issues in Maritime Cyber Security

A Different Dimension: Reflections on the History of Transpersonal Thought

Iran: Who Is Really In Charge?

Contracting, Logistics, Reverse Logistics: The Project, Program and Portfolio Approach

Unworkable Conservatism: Small Government, Freemarkets, and Impracticality

Springfield: The Novel

Lariats and Lassos

Ongoing Issues in Georgian Policy and Public Administration

Growing Inequality: Bridging Complex Systems, Population Health and Health Disparities

Designing, Adapting, Strategizing in Online Education

Pacific Hurtgen: The American Army in Northern Luzon, 1945

Natural Gas as an Instrument of Russian State Power

New Frontiers in Criminology

Feeding the Global South

Beijing Express: How to Understand New China

The Rise of the Book Plate: An Exemplative of the Art

Bedouins

Mary Garden, Idols and Ambergris

by James Huneker

WESTPHALIA PRESS
An Imprint of Policy Studies Organization

Bedouins, Mary Garden, Idols, and Ambergris
All Rights Reserved © 2018 by Policy Studies Organization

Westphalia Press
An imprint of Policy Studies Organization
1527 New Hampshire Ave., NW
Washington, D.C. 20036
info@ipsonet.org

ISBN-13: 978-1-63391-658-6
ISBN-10: 1-63391-658-8

Cover design by Jeffrey Barnes:
jbarnesbook.design

Daniel Gutierrez-Sandoval, Executive Director
PSO and Westphalia Press

Updated material and comments on this edition
can be found at the Westphalia Press website:
www.westphaliapress.org

BEDOUINS

From a photograph by De Meyer

MARY GARDEN—HERSELF

BEDOUINS

MARY GARDEN, DEBUSSY,
CHOPIN OR THE CIRCUS, BOTTICELLI, POE, BRAHMSODY,
ANATOLE FRANCE, MIRBEAU, CARUSO ON WHEELS,
CALICO CATS, THE ARTISTIC TEMPERAMENT;
IDOLS AND AMBERGRIS; WITH THE SUPREME SIN,
GRINDSTONES, A MASQUE OF MUSIC, AND
THE VISION MALEFIC

BY
JAMES HUNEKER

WITH VARIOUS PORTRAITS OF MARY GARDEN IN
OPERATIC COSTUME

NEW YORK
CHARLES SCRIBNER'S SONS
1920

COPYRIGHT, 1920, BY
CHARLES SCRIBNER'S SONS

Published February, 1920

COPYRIGHT, 1919, BY THE NEW YORK TIMES CO.
COPYRIGHT, 1918, BY THE ESS ESS PUBLISHING CO.
COPYRIGHT, 1917, BY THE SUN PRINTING & PUBLISHING ASSN.

THIS BOOK OF BEDOUINS
IS DEDICATED

"À la très-belle, à la très-bonne, à la très-chère."

"J'aime mieux le désert, je retourne chez les Bédouins qui sont libres . . . ."
Gustave Flaubert.

"The Bedouins camp within Pharaoh's palace walls, and the old war-ship is given over to the rats."
Robert Louis Stevenson.

CONTENTS

PART I—MARY GARDEN

CHAPTER		PAGE
I.	SUPERWOMAN	3
II.	INTIMATE	15
III.	THE BABY, THE CRITIC, AND THE GUITAR	21
IV.	INTERPRETER	30
V.	MÉLISANDE AND DEBUSSY	45
VI.	THE ARTISTIC TEMPERAMENT	53
VII.	THE PASSING OF OCTAVE MIRBEAU	64
VIII.	ANARCHS AND ECSTASY	73
IX.	PAINTED MUSIC	81
X.	POE AND HIS POLISH CONTEMPORARY	94
XI.	GEORGE LUKS	106
XII.	CONCERNING CALICO CATS	118
XIII.	CHOPIN OR THE CIRCUS?	125
XIV.	CARUSO ON WHEELS	134
XV.	SING AND GROW VOICELESS	144
XVI.	ANATOLE FRANCE: THE LAST PHASE	154
XVII.	A MASQUE OF MUSIC	164

CONTENTS

PART II—IDOLS AND AMBERGRIS

CHAPTER		PAGE
I.	THE SUPREME SIN	177
II.	BROTHERS-IN-LAW	201
III.	GRINDSTONES	216
IV.	VENUS OR VALKYR?	225
V.	THE CARDINAL'S FIDDLE	247
VI.	RENUNCIATION	256
VII.	THE VISION MALEFIC	261

ILLUSTRATIONS

Mary Garden—Herself	*Frontispiece*
	FACING PAGE
Rosina Galli	24
Mary Garden as Mélisande	34
Mary Garden as Monna Vanna	38
Mary Garden as Salome	78
Rosina Galli as the Princess in "Le Coq d'Or"	140

PART I
MARY GARDEN

I

SUPERWOMAN

LA BEAUTÉ

"Je suis belle, ô mortels! comme un rêve de pierre,
Et mon sein, où chacun s'est meurtri tour à tour,
Est fait pour inspirer au poëte un amour
Éternel et meut, ainsi, que la matière."
. . . .
       —*Charles Baudelaire.*

THAT little girl down Boston way, who had mastered William James and Boris Sidis before she was in her teens, behaved badly one afternoon. Possibly it was the sultry weather, or growing pains—in the psychic sphere, of course—or, perhaps, it may have been due to the reflexes from prolonged attention to the Freudian psycho-analysis and the significance of Twilight Sleep; but whatever the cause, that precocious child flew off her serene handle and literally "sassed" the entire household. The tantrum over—she afterward described it as a uric-acid storm—and order reigning once more in Bach Bay, she was severely interrogated by her male parent as to the whys and wherefores of her singular deviation from accustomed glacial intellectual objectivity. Her answer was in the proper key: "My multiple personalities failed to co-ordinate. Hence the distressing lack of centripetal functioning." She was immediately forgiven. Multiple personalities are to blame for much in this vale of tears; that is, if you are unlucky or lucky enough to be possessed of the seven devils of psychology.

Mary Garden was, no doubt, a naughty little girl in her time. That she climbed trees, fought boys twice her size, stuck out her tongue at pious folk, scandalized her parents, and tore from the heads of nice girls handfuls of hair, I am sure. Hedda Gabler thus treated gentle Thea Elvstad in the play. But was this demon Mary aware of her multiple personalities? Of her complexes? Her art fusion is such perfect synthesis. Subconscious is nowadays an excuse for the Original Sin with which we are saddled by theologians.

Well, one bad turn deserves another, and we may easily picture the wild Scottish thistle defiantly shrugging shoulders at law and order. She did not analyze her Will-to-Raise-Merry-Hell. No genius of her order ever does. There had been signs and omens. Her mother before her birth had dreamed wonderful dreams; dreamed and prayed that she might become a singer. But even maternal intuition could not have foreseen such a swan triumphantly swimming through the troubled waters of life. A swan, did I say? A condor, an eagle, a peacock, a nightingale, a panther, a society dame, a gallery of moving-pictures, a siren, an indomitable

MARY GARDEN

fighter, a human woman with a heart as big as a house, a lover of sport, an electric personality, and a canny Scotch lassie who can force from an operatic manager wails of anguish because of her close bargaining over a contract; in a word, a Superwoman.

My dear friend and master, the late Remy de Gourmont, wrote that man differs from his fellow animals—he didn't say "lower"—because of the diversity of his aptitudes. Man is not the only organism that shows multiple personalities; even in plant life pigmentation and the power of developing new species prove that our vaunted superiorities are only relative. I may refer you to the experiments of Hugo de Vriès at the Botanical Gardens, Amsterdam, where the grand old Dutch scientist presented me with sixteen-leaf clover naturally developed, and grown between sunset and dawn; also an evening primrose—Æonthera Lamarckiana—which shoots into new flowers. Multiple personalities again. In the case of Mary Garden we call her artistic aptitudes "the gift of versatility." All distinguished actresses have this serpent-like facility of shedding their skin and taking on a fresh one at will. She is Cleopatra—with "serpent and scarab for sign"—or Mélisande, Phryne, or Monna Vanna; as Thaïs she is both saint and courtesan, her Salome breeds horror; and in the simplicities of Jean the Juggler of Notre Dame a Mary Garden, hitherto submerged, appears: tender, boyish, sweet, fantastic;

a ray of moonshine has entered his head and made of him an irresponsible yet irresistibly charming youth.

Not without warrant is Karma believed in by people whose imagination cannot be penned behind the bars of Now. Before to-day was yesterday, and to traverse that Eternal Corridor of Time has been the fate of mankind. The Eternal Return—rather say, the Eternal Recommencement—mad as it seems, is not to be made mock of. It is always the same pair of eyes that peer through windows opening on infinity. What the Karmas of Mary Garden? In spirit-land what avatars! Is she the reincarnation of that Phryne of the "splendid scarlet sins," or the Faustine who crowded into a moment the madness of joy and crime; or the recrudescence of a Sapho who turned her back on the Leucadian promontory, turned from the too masculine Phaon and sought her Anactoria, sought and wooed her with lyric sighs; has she recaptured, this extraordinary Mary of Aberdeen, the soul of Aspasia, who beguiled Pericles and artistic Athens with the sinuous irony of the serpent; and Gismonda, Louise, and Violetta, all those subtle sonorous sinners—was she in her anterior existence any or all of them? Did she know the glory that was Greece, the grandeur that was Rome? Henry James has warned us not to ask of an author why he selects a particular subject for treatment. It is a dangerous question to put; the answer might prove

MARY GARDEN

disconcerting. And with Miss Garden the same argument holds. Her preference for certain characters is probably dictated by reasons obscure even to herself. With her the play-instinct is imperious; it dominates her daylight hours, it overflows into her dream-life. Again the sounding motive of multiple personalities, Karma, subconsciousness, the profound core of human nature. And on the palette of her art there is the entire gamut of tones, from passionate purple to the iridescent delicacies of iris-grey.

That Mary Garden interprets a number of widely differentiated characters is a critical platitude. Chapter and verse might be given for her excellences as well as her defects. Nor does she depend upon any technical formula or formulas. Versatility is her brevet of distinction. An astounding versatility. Now, the ways and means of the acting-singer are different from actors in the theatre. Dramatic values are altered. The optique of the opera shifts the stock attitudes, gestures, poses, and movements into another and more magnified dimension. Victor Maurel, master of all singing-actors, employed a sliding scale of values in his delineation of De Nevers, Don Giovanni, Iago, and Falstaff. His power of characterization enabled him to portray a Valentine true to type, nevertheless individual; and if there is a more banal figure on the operatic boards than Valentine, we do not know his name (perhaps

Faust . . .!). But every year the space that separates the lyric from the dramatic stage is shrinking. Richard Wagner was not the first composer to stress action; he is the latest, however, whose influence has been tremendously far-reaching. He insisted that the action should suit the singing word. To-day acting and singing are inextricably blended, and I can conceive of nothing more old-fashioned and outmoded than the Wagnerian music-drama as interpreted in the dramatic terms of the old Wagnerian singers. They walked, rather waddled, through the mystic mazes of the score, shouted or screamed the music, and generally were prodigious bores—except when Lilli Lehmann sang. After all, Wagner must be sung. When Jean de Reszke pictured a Tristan—a trifle of the carpet-knight —he both sang and acted. It was the beginning of the New Wagner, a totally changed Wagner, else his music-drama will remain in dusty pigeonholes. Debussy has sounded the modern key.

There is born, or reborn—nothing is new since the early Florentines—a New Opera, and in its train new methods of interpretation. Merely to sing well is as futile as attempting to act though voiceless. The modern trend is away from melodrama, whether Italian, French, or German; away from its antique, creaking machinery. Debussy patterned after Wagner for a time and then blazed new paths. As Serge Prokofieff so acutely observed to me: "In Pel-

MARY GARDEN

léas and Mélisande Debussy rewrote Tristan and Isolde." The emotional scale is transposed to fewer dynamic values and rhythms made more subtle; the action is shown as in a dream. The play's the thing, and reality is muffled. Elsewhere we have studied the Mélisande of Mary Garden. Like her Monna Vanna, it reveals the virtues and shortcomings of the New Opera. Too static for popular taste, it is nevertheless an escape from the tyranny of operatic convention. Like the rich we shall always have "grand opera" with us. It is the pabulum of the unmusical, the unthinking, the tasteless. Its theatricalisms are more depressing than Sardou's. The quintessence of art, or the arts, which the modern Frenchmen, above all, the new Russian composers (from the mighty Slavic races may come the artistic, perhaps the religious salvation of the world—for I am a believer in Dostoievsky's, not Tolstoy's, Christianity), are distilling into their work is for more auditors than the "ten superior persons scattered throughout the universe" of whom Huysmans wrote. There is a growing public that craves, demands, something different from the huge paraphernalia of crudely colored music, scenery, costume, lath and plaster, and vociferous singing. Oh, the dulness, the staleness, the brutal obviousness of it all! Every cadence with its semaphoric signalling, every phrase and its accompanying gesture. Poetry is slain at a stroke, the ear promise-crammed, but imagination goes hungry. The New Art—an art of precious essences, an evocation, an enchantment of the senses, a sixth sense—is our planetary ideal.

And in the New Opera Mary Garden is the supreme exemplar. She sounds the complex modern note. She does not represent, she evokes. She sings and she acts, and the densely woven web is impossible to disentangle. Her Gaelic temperament is of an intensity; she is white-hot, a human dynamo with sudden little retorsions that betray a tender, sensitive soul, through the brilliant, hard shell of an emerald personality; she is also the opal, with it chameleonic hues. Her rhythms are individual. Her artistic evolution may be traced. She stems from the Gallic theatre. She has studied Sarah Bernhardt and Yvette Guilbert—the perfect flowering of the "diseuse"—but she pins her faith to the effortless art of Eleonora Duse. The old contention that stirred Coquelin and Henry Irving does not interest her so much as does Duse. We have discussed the Coquelin-Irving crux: should an actor leave nothing to chance or should he improvise on the spur of high emotions?—that is what the question comes to. Miss Garden denied her adherence either to Coquelin or Irving. I asked her to give us a peep into her artistic cuisine while she prepared her sauces. Notwithstanding her refusal to let us participate in the brewing of her magic broth, I still believe that she sided with

MARY GARDEN

Coquelin. She is eminently cerebral. And yet her chief appeal is to the imagination. Not a stroke of her camel's-hair brush, not the boldest massing of colors, are left to chance. She knows the flaming way she came, she knows the misty return. Not a tone of her naturally rich, dark voice but takes on the tinting of the situation. This doesn't forbid a certain latitude for temperamental variations, which are plentiful at each of her performances. She knows tempo rubato and its value in moods. She has mastered, too, the difficult quality described by William Gillette as the First-time Illusion in Acting. Various are the Mary Gardens in her map of art.

And she is ours. Despite her Scottish birth she has remained invincibly Yankee. Despite long residence in her beloved Paris, enough American has rubbed off on her, and the resilient, dynamic, overflowing, and proud spirit that informs her art and character are American or nothing. Race counts. Can any good come out of our Nazareth of art? The answer is inevitable: Yes, Mary Garden. She is Our Mary. Lyrically, dramatically ours, yet an orchid. Dear old Flaubert forcibly objected to Sarah Bernhardt being called "a social expression." But she was, and this despite her Dutch ancestry and the exotic strain in her blood. Miss Garden may not emphasize her American side, but it is the very skeleton of her artistic organism. Would that an Aubrey Beardsley lived to note in evanescent traceries her potent personality, a rare something that arouses the "emotion of recognition," but which we cannot define. "Come," said Berlioz to Legouvé in the early years of the third decade of the last century. "I am going to let you see something which you have never seen, and some one whom you shall never forget." Berlioz meant the playing and personality of Frédéric Chopin. Garden is leagues asunder from Chopin—who was the rarest apparition of his age; but as an interpretative artist she is rare enough for sympathetic writers to embalm in the amber of their pagan prose; definitely to pin to their pages this gorgeous dragon-fly.

Another bribe to her audience is the beauty of Mary Garden. But I do not wish here to dwell upon its value in her unforgettable portrayals of the dear dead grand ladies, the stately courtesans of the dim past. Stéphane Mallarmé wrote a poem, though not in verse, depicting a crowd assembled in the canvas house of the Interpreter of Past Things.

George Moore thus Englished "The Future Phenomenon." A showman tells the despairing, ugly men and women of his wonderful prize. "No sign regales you of the spectacle within, for there is not now a painter capable of presenting any sad shadow of it. I bring alive (and preserved through the years by sovereign science) a woman of old time. Some folly, original and simple, in ecstasy of gold, I know not what

MARY GARDEN

she names it, her hair falls with the grace of rich stuffs about her face and contrasts with the blood-like nudity of her lips. In place of her vain gown she has a body; and her eyes, though like rare stones, are not worth the look that leaps from the happy flesh; the breasts, raised as if filled with an eternal milk, are pointed to the sky, and the smooth limbs still keep the salt of the primal sea. . . ." You think of fair-haired Mélisande as she exquisitely murmurs her pathetic "Je ne suis pas heureuse ici."

Some years ago in Paris I saw and heard the Garden Traviata. The singing was superlative; she then boasted a coloratura style that would surprise those who now only know her vocalization. It was, however, the conception and acting that intrigued me. Originality stamped both. The death scene was of unusual poignancy; evidently the young American had been spying upon Bernhardt and Duse. This episode adumbrated the marvellous death of Mélisande, the most touching that I can recall in either the lyric or dramatic theatre. It is a pity that she cannot find sterner stuff than Massenet, Leroux, Fevrier, and the rest of that puff-paste decorative school. There are composers, too, of more vital calibre than Camille Erlanger. Debussy is a master; but there must be newer men who could view Mary Garden as the ideal exponent of their music. Meanwhile, she has discovered a rôle in which she would pique the curiosity of the most uncritical mossbacks. She has added Isolde to her long list. Mary Garden and Isolde! Incredible! Nevertheless, an interesting experiment this if she could be persuaded to voice the sorrows of the Irish Princess. It would be no longer Wagner. It would suffer a rich sea-change. Wagner muted, perhaps Wagner undone; certainly unsung if we remember glorious Olive Fremstad. But a magical Isolde, with more than a hint of the perversely exotic we feel in Aubrey Beardsley's drawings of Isolde and Tristan. The modern note again. Beardsley paraphrasing Botticelli; Watteau plucking at the robe of Rubens; Debussy smiting the chords of Wagner. Such an Isolde would be too bewildering to be true.

II

INTIMATE

"Et on fait la guerre avec de la musique, des panaches,
des drapeaus, des hanches d'or. . . ."
—*Tentation de Saint Antoine* (*slightly altered*).

THE penalty of publicity is one which singers seldom evade. Little need to give the reason, nevertheless, for sensitive souls it is a trial to see one's personality put in the wash, squeezed, and hung up to dry with other linen in the pitiless laundry of the press. Some singers are born advertisers, some achieve advertising, but few have advertising thrust upon them. That sort usually fade into shadow-land rather than face the fierce white light which beats about the operatic throne. Really, it must be disconcerting for a woman singer to hear herself discussed as if she were a race-horse. Every point in her make-up is put on a platter ready to serve hot in the newspapers. You fancy yourself overhearing the conversation of jockeys and trainers. "Oi sye, Bill, that there filly is goin' queer. Jest look at her fetlocks, and her crupper is gettin' too heavy. Take her out for an hour's spin on the downs. Breathe her a bit and then give her a hard sweatin' run and a rub down. No water, Bill, mind ye, or I'll knock yer block off."

The private life of a prima donna is not unlike that of a racing mare's. Flesh reduction, with all the succulent food—and champagne—are banished; indulgence spells decadence, and decadence is eagerly noted by the psychic detectives known as music-critics. We are not in the game to find fault as simple souls imagine, but to register values, vocal and personal. It's a pity, but this is a condition and not a theory. We have heard of a Mary Garden cult. Now, as has been said by Dr. Wicksteed, a cult is always annoying to those who do not join in it, and generally hurtful to those who do. But is there such a Garden cult? We doubt it. She has a certain elect following, and for those admirers she can do no wrong. She has aroused the critical antagonism of some who, rightly enough, point out her obvious limitations. To these the gruff reply of Brahms is appropriate. A presuming youth called his attention to a theme in a work of his which was evidently borrowed from Mendelssohn. "That any fool can see," said the crusty Johannes. The voice of Miss Garden is sometimes a voice in the wilderness: sandy, harsh, yet expressive. The same may be said of Geraldine Farrar, who every year is gravitating toward the zone, not of silence, but of the singing-actress. A Gallic, not an Italian zone. Voice does not play the major rôle; acting, that is, dramatic character-

MARY GARDEN

ization, does. Not to recognize in Miss Garden the quintessence of this art—not altogether a new one, and its most perfect flowering is the art of Yvette Guilbert—is to miss the real Mary Garden. Voilà tout! We saw a like misunderstanding of Eleonora Duse. Immediately she was compared, and unfavorably, with Sarah Bernhardt, when she was achieving something vastly different, and, I think, vastly finer. Sarah was more brilliant, Duse more human; the one an orchestra, the other an exquisitely balanced string quartet. Mary Garden is the nearest approach to Duse on the lyric stage.

Mary Garden, too, is "different," in the sense Stendhal meant that banal word. Her cadenced speech is not singing in the Italian manner. To begin with, her tonal texture is not luscious. But there are compensations. Every phrase is charged with significance. She paints with her voice, and if her palette is composed of the cooler tones, if the silver-greys and sombre greens of a Velasquez predominate, it is because she needs just such a gamut with which to load her brush. She is a consummate manipulator of values. To be sure, we do not expect the torrential outbursts of Margaret Matzenauer. Why confuse two antithetical propositions? I don't look at one of the Paul Cézannes in the rare collection of Miss Lillie Bliss expecting the gorgeous hues of a Monticelli. Cézanne is a master of values. And if these similes seem far-fetched—which they are not; music and color are twins in the Seven Arts—then let us pitch upon a more homely illustration: Mary Garden is an opal, Margaret Matzenauer a full-blown rose. Voltaire said that the first man who compared a woman to a rose was a poet; the second, an ass. I hope Mme. Matzenauer will accept the simile in the poetic sense.

Nuance, which alone makes art or life endurable, becomes an evocation with Miss Garden. I lament that she is not in a more intimate setting, as the misted fire and rhythmic modulations of her opaline art and personality are lost in such a huge auditorium as the Lexington Theatre. I saw her, a slip of a girl, at Paris, early in this century, and framed by the Opéra Comique, of whose traditions she is now the most distinguished exponent. She was then something precious: a line of Pater's prose, the glance of one of Da Vinci's strange ladies; a chord by Debussy; honey, tiger's blood, and absinthe; or like the enigmatic pallor we see in Renaissance portraits; cruel, voluptuous, and suggesting the ennui of Watteau's L'Indifférent.

She is all things to all critics.

There are those who see in her the fascinating woman. And they are justified in their belief. There are those who discover in her something disquieting, ambiguous; one of Baudelaire's "femmes damnées" from whom he fashioned his Beethovenian harmonies, fulgurating, profound: "Descendez le chemin de l'enfer éternel! . . . flagellés par un vent qui ne vient pas du ciel."

MARY GARDEN

... And there is still another group to which I adhere, one that envisages Mary in the more lucid light of an admirable artist, who has fashioned of her body and soul a rare instrument, giving forth the lovely music of attitude, gesture, pose, and rhythm. There are moments when she evokes the image of the shadow of a humming-bird on a star; and often she sounds the shuddering semitones of sex, as in Thaïs. The Mélisande moods are hers, the dim, remote poesy of antique sonorous tapestries; and the "modern" note of Louise, grazing the vulgar, though purified by passion. But the dissenters no doubt believe in the Cambodian proverb when estimating the singing of both Geraldine Farrar and Mary Garden. It runs thus: When in hades it is bad form to speak of the heat.

Do you remember the night when Mary Garden came from the refectory of the monastery in Le Jongleur, and—oh, the winsome little devil!—paused on the stairway to remark to her audience: "La cuisine est très bonne"?

The accent was indescribable. At Paris they admired her individual French streaked with exotic intonations. That night it revealed the universal accent of a half-starved lad who had just filled his tummy; a real "tuck-out." The joy of life! How human she was! It is the sartorial technique of Miss Garden that is supreme. Her taste in costumes is impeccable. In the eternal game of making masculine eyes misbehave, she is quite irresistible. But this orchidaceous Circe, this uncommon or garden variety, does not with her fatal philtres transform men into the unmentionable animal; rather does she cause them to scurry after their vocabulary and lift up their voices in rhetorical praise. And that is something to have accomplished. Did you ever read Casuals of the Sea, by William McFee, a fiction I had the honor to introduce to the American reading public? On page 443 there occurs at the chapter end the following dialogue: "Mother!" "Yes, Minnie." "Mother, I was just thinking what fools men are! What utter fools! But oh, mother, dear mother, what fools we are, not to find it out—sooner!" Minnie had seen a bit of life on the Continent; she was then snug in the landlocked harbor of stagnant matrimonial waters. But she understood men. Miss Garden is a profounder philosopher than Minnie Briscoe. She knew her public "sooner," and the result is —Mary Garden. Qui a bu, boira!

I have been asked whether Miss Garden believes that she is the wonderful artiste I believe her to be. I really don't know. But I feel assured that if she discovers she does not measure up to all the qualities ascribed to her she will promptly develop them; such is the plastic, involutionary force of this extraordinary woman.

III
THE BABY, THE CRITIC, AND THE GUITAR

GEORGE SAINTSBURY, that blunt literary critic who always called a cat a cat, wrote a study of Charles Baudelaire in an English magazine at least forty years ago. It practically introduced the poet to English readers, although Swinburne had imported no little of the "poisonous honey from France" in Laus Veneris. Prof. Saintsbury told of a friend to whom he had shown the etching of François Flameng after Herrera's The Baby and the Guitar. "So," said the friend, "you like this picture. I always thought you hated babies!" The remark is a classic example of that sin against the holy ghost of criticism, the confusion of two widely varying intellectual substances; a mixing up of the babies with a vengeance. The anecdote may serve to point a moral if not to adorn my sermon.

The operatic undertow of the past season cast up strange flotsam and jetsam and derelicts, usually in the shape of letters. Letters signed and unsigned. Two I select as illustrating the Baby and the Guitar crux. I stand for the Baby and two celebrated singing girls represent the Guitar. Both letters are unsigned, both reveal a woman's handwriting, though different women. The first roundly accuses the dignified author of being madly in love with Mary Garden; the second wonders why I worship Margaret Matzenauer. Now, the venerable age of the present alleged and versatile "great lover" —Leo Ditrichstein should look to his laurels!— might serve as an implicit denial of these charges, were it not the fact that there are hoary-headed sinners abroad seeking whom they may devour. If I were a young chap I should pay no attention, but being as old as I am I proudly confess my crimes, merely pausing to ask, who isn't in love with Mary Garden and Margaret Matzenauer? Their audiences, to an unprejudiced eye, seem to be very much so, men, women, and children alike. Why not that worm-of-all-work, the music-critic? We, too, have feelings like any other humans. But worse follows. A sympathetic singer sent me a telegram which read thus: "Why doesn't your wife put you behind bars?" to which I promptly replied, Celtic fashion, by asking another question: "Which one?" meaning, of course, which bar. Here is a concrete case of the Baby and the Guitar muddle. One can't praise the art of Mary Garden without loving the woman! One can't admire the opulent voice of Margaret Matzenauer without being dragged a hopeless slave at her triumphant chariot wheels; a critic butchered to make a prima donna's holiday! Absurd!

MARY GARDEN

And there are others. What of radiant Geraldine with the starry eyes? What of Frieda Hempel, exquisite Violetta, delicious Countess in the Rose-Cavalier? And what of Olive Fremstad, always beautiful, an Isolde whose tenderness is without peer, a Sieglinde who plucks at your heartstrings because of her pity-breeding loveliness, or as that dazzling witch, Kundry; and to whose beauty the years have lent a tragic, expressive mask? There were queens, too, before Agamemnon's. Lilli Lehmann, Emma Eames, Lillian Nordica, Emma Calvé—did we not burn incense under the nostrils of those beautiful women and great artists? Go to! Nor was our praise accorded only to the girls of yesteryear. The De Reszkes, Victor Maurel, Max Alvary—as perfect a type of the matinée idol as Harry Montague or Charles Coghlan—the stately, if slightly frigid, Pol Plançon—upon them we showered our warmest enthusiasms. And Ignace Jan Paderewski, once Premier Opus I of Poland—was he neglected? The piano god par excellence. No, such generalizations are unfair. The average music-critic or dramatic critic is nothing if not versatile in his tastes. Remember that either one has opportunities to see and hear the most comely faces and sweetest voices. Nevertheless I know of none who ever lost his head. We play no favorites. I also admit that this apologetic tone is the kind of excuse that is accusatory. But ——!

But there is another name which slipped the

memory of my faultfinders. What of Rosina Galli, whose pedal technique is as perfect as the vocal technique of Miss Hempel; whose mimique is as wonderful in its way as are the hieratic attitudes and patibulary gestures of Mary, the celebrated serpent of Old Nile? Don't we, to a man, adore Rosina? Thunderous affirmations assail the welkin! And then there is the "poet's secret," as Bernard Shaw, the "Uncle Gurnemanz" of British politics, has it. The secret in question is as simple as Polchinelle's. Do you realize that to a writer interested in his art such women as Mary Garden or Margaret Matzenauer serve as a peg for his polyphonic prose or as models upon which to drape his cloth-of-silver when writing of Geraldine Farrar? A susceptible critic may perforce sigh like a symphonic furnace, but apart from such fatuities he can't keep up the excitement without a lot of emotional stoking. And coal is so costly this year. That alone negates the assertion of undue sentimentality. Pooh! I shouldn't give a hang for a critic so cold that he couldn't write overheated prose, Byzantine prose, purple-patched and swaggeringly rhythmed, when facing these golden girls. "Passionate press agents," indeed, but in the strict sense intended when Philip Hale struck off that memorial phrase. There is Pitts Sanborn with his "lithe moon-blonde wonderful Mary," which I envy him; after my spilth of adjectives he limns in five words the garden-goddess, Themes, those singers, for gorgeous

From a photograph by De Strelecki

ROSINA GALLI

MARY GARDEN

vocables; nothing more. Footlight-prose quickly forgotten if you take from the shelf in your library the beloved essays of Cardinal Newman and swim in the cool currents of his silvery style. A panacea for the strained, morbid, fantastic atmosphere of grand opera.

A character in one of Goethe's novels—Wilhelm Meister?—exclaims: "Five minutes more of this and I confess everything!" Another such season of overwrought reportage and my bag of highly colored phrases, all my trick adjectives, would be exhausted, else gone stale, and the same gang of girls ever expecting new and more miraculous homage in four languages with a brass band around the corner. Oh! la! la!

There was one critic that did fall in love with an actress. His name is Hector Berlioz, and he celebrated the charms of Henrietta Smithson, English born, a "guest" at a Parisian theatre, by passionately pounding the kettle-drums in the orchestra. His amatory tattoo, coupled with his flaming locks, finally attracted the lady's attention, and after she broke her leg and was forced to abandon the stage she had her revenge —she married the kettle-drum critic and composer, and lived unhappily ever afterward. Yet the feeling against critics persists, probably prompted by envy. In a Dublin theatre gallery a fight broke out, and one chap was getting the worst of it. His more powerful adversary was pushing him over the rail into the orchestra, when a wag called out: "Don't waste him. Kill

BEDOUINS

a fiddler with him!" Nowadays he would say, "Kill a critic." But sufferance is the badge of our tribe. There are times when I long for the unaffected charm of Heller rather than Chopin; when I prefer to gaze at Wagner's Grane rather than hear Brunhilde sing.

Mary Garden makes herself beautiful, if only by thinking "beautiful." "Whatever happens, I must be an emerald," said Antoninus of the emerald's morality. Havelock Ellis asserts, "the exquisite things of life are to-day as rare and as precious as ever they were." She is rare and precious in Mélisande, Monna Vanna, Jean, and other rôles. And what imaginative intensity is hers! But I don't care a fig for the depraved creatures of the Lower Empire she so marvellously portrays. It is Mary with the strain of mysticism, the woodland fay she shows us, its nascent soul modulating into the supreme suffering and sorrow of motherhood. Her bed of death in Mélisande is one of the high consolations in the memory of a critic whose existence has been spent in the quagmire of mediocrity. In the kingdom of the mystics there are many mansions, and Garden lives in one—at times.

But the détraqué lemans she pictures are often repugnant. The decadent art of Byzance. The Infernal Feminine. A vase exquisitely carved containing corruption. Sculptured slime. You close your eyes—but open your fingers; the temptation to peep is irresistible.

In his illuminative studies of Fremstad, Far-

MARY GARDEN

rar, Garden, Mazarin, Interpreters and Interpretations, Carl Van Vechten says that to Miss Garden a wig is the all-important thing. "Once I have donned the wig of a character, I am that character. It would be difficult for me to go on the stage in my own hair." However, she did so in Louise, adds the critic. Felix Orman reports that when he asked her if she would be content to give up singing and become a dramatic artist, she replied: "No. I need the music. I depend on it. Music is my medium of expression." An art amphibian, hybrid, hers. The flying fish. The bird that swims. The dubious trail of the epicene is not a modern note. Rome and Alexandria knew it. It is vile, soulless, yet fascinating. Miss Garden incarnates it as no other modern since the divine Sarah. She is "cérébrale," and a cerebral is defined by Arthur Symons as one who feels with the head and thinks with the heart. Richard Strauss is a prime exemplar. The image suggests both apoplexy and angina pectoris, yet it serves. She is as hard as steel in Louise or Cléopâtre, yet how melting as Monna and Mélisande. She may be heartless for all I know, and that is in her favor, artistically considered, for Steeplejack hath enjoined: A cool head and a wicked heart will conquer the world; also, what shall it profit a woman if she saves her soul but loseth love? Cynical Steeplejack? Yet, a half-truth—though not the upper half of that shy goddess, Truth.

As for Margaret Matzenauer, her art and personality transport the imagination to more exotic climes. That sombre and magnificent woman, who seems to have stepped from a fresco of Hans Makart, himself a follower of Paolo Veronese, is a singing Caterina Cornaro. She brought back an element of lyric grandeur to our pale operatic life; a Judith, a Deborah, Boadicea, Belkis, Clytemnestra, Dalila, Amneris, or Aholibah, all those splendid tragic shapes of the antique world, she evokes, and in her singing there is a largeness of dramatic utterance that proclaims her of the line royal: Lehmann, Brandt, Ternina, Fremstad, Schumann-Heink. Is it at all remarkable that I admire Matzenauer?

And now that we have cleared away some cobwebs of misapprehension with the aid of the Baby and the Guitar, let me relate a story of Châteaubriand, that Eternal Philanderer, as I once named him, who met at Rome gay Hortense Allart, afterward Madame Meritens. The supreme master of French prose regretfully exclaimed to her: "Ah, if I had back my fifty years." Thereupon the sprightly lady replied: "Why not wish for twenty-five?" "No," moodily returned the Ambassador, "fifty will do." Which recalls the witty design of Forain, representing a very old man apostrophizing the shadow of his past: "Oh, if I only had again my sixty-five years!" I should be glad to have my threescore and ten if only to tell those great ladies of opera how much I admire them. "Barkis is willin'."

MARY GARDEN

Another picture and I shall have done. Listen. I, many years ago, visited the Fondation Ste. Perine at Auteuil, an institution endowed by the Empress Eugénie, one in which the benevolence is so cloaked as not to hurt the sensibilities of the resident superannuated ladies and gentlemen. The company boasted noble origins. Among the ladies I met was a Polish-born Marquise, with brilliant eyes and wonderful white hair, her own. She had studied with Chopin. She said he was fickle and that George Sand was often jealous of his pupils. For me she sang in a sweet, true, but quavering voice Chopin's Maiden's Wish, and compelled tears. The Marquise then tinkled with a still small tone a Nocturne by Field upon a pianoforte whose ivory keys looked as if they exhaled pearly sighs. She gently coquetted with a touch of exquisite Sarmatian evasiveness. For me she was adorable, although if she had laughed her face would have cracked its artistic plastering. What a new Diana of Poitiers! What wit, fire, malice, were in the glance of her soft, faded blue eyes! What a magically youthful heart! She must have been more than fourscore.

But yet a woman.

IV

INTERPRETER

TO MARY GARDEN AS CLEOPATRA
"C'est Affreux Mourir"

"And now this scorchèd terrace is your sole domain,
  Your only subject Roman, dying Anthony;
  The outer vastnesses they held, the soldiery
Of Cæsar; their stout captain will not here refrain.

You lived, O Queen, but not to countenance that pain
  Which is surrender of the body's sovereignty;
  You take your part; is it the frightful thing to die
And see in dying just the realm you must regain?

You have not let the game play you, my Queen, but fed
  The aspic at a famished breast—the rascal fresh
  From gluttony a glutton still!—Why, the hot land
Is dim, alone lies Anthony save for the dead—
  One more ambition, Queen, for your expiring hand.
  The last adventure, woman of imperious flesh!"
                               —*Pitts Sanborn.*

CLEOPATRA

THOUGH the first hearing of the work in New York was during the winter of 1919 at the Lexington Theatre, and sung by the Chicago Opera Association, Cleofonte Campanini, director, it had been presented before Chicago audiences when the impersonation of the supersubtle serpent of Old Nile by Mary Garden caused much comment, critical and otherwise. The libretto states that the conception of M. Payen radically differs from Shakespeare's tragedy—a rather superfluous remark. It does considerably differ, the principal difference being that Shakespeare wrote great poetry as well as great drama.

Payen's attempt resolves itself into a series of tableaux, the characterization generalized, his verse respectably tepid. In a word, not the Queen that Shakespeare drew. Of this Cléopâtre you dare not say: "Age cannot wither her, nor custom stale her infinite variety." She is more germane to that Queen shown us in the sumptuous prose of Theophile Gautier's Une Nuit de Cléopâtre than the imperial courtesan who turned the head of Anthony and stirred the pulse of Julius Cæsar to the supreme tune of Shakespeare's music.

There is plenty of action, some picturesque episodes, and at least one brutal scene. Of love and the talk of love there is no end. Yet it is not all convincing. Moving pictures. You think of Gérôme, of Le Nouy, of the hundred and one painters who have celebrated on canvas this seductive creature of old Egypt. "For her own person, it beggar'd all description; she did lie in her pavillon, cloth-of-gold of tissue, o'er-picturing that Venus where we see the fancy out-work nature."

Cléopâtre is Massenet and the modiste. Brackish-sweet, it is the ultimate expression of musical impotence. Clever craftsman Massehet could turn out martial music and amorous, the clangor of trumpets and voluptuous, dizzy dance measures. But here it is generally bosh. Languid, enervating, it attained a feeble climax in the ballet of the penultimate act. Ambiguous shapes and attitudes crowded the scene. Two dancers slipped and fell, but the recovery was so swift that the tumbled ensemble seemed a veritable climax. Cléopâtre cynically regarded this daring symbolism, though Marc-Antoine seemed rather shocked. And he should have been. Musically speaking, nothing happened in Act I; less followed in Act II, while Act III was a glittering triumph of vacuity. In the last act the asp played protagonist. As its name did not figure on the programme, it probably died from envy, or else inanition, doubtless humming Will Shakespeare's mournful lay: "I am dying, Egypt, dying." You also recall Swinburne's: "Under those low, large lids of hers She hath the histories of all times. . . ."

But the Cléopâtre! A youthful Sphinx, her entrance on the great burnished barge was an evocation. As she faced Antoine so must have looked Sheba's Queen before the majesty of Solomon. It would have been trying on the nerves of the most pudic potentate from Herod down. A saucy lad, in a later scene, Cléopâtre got in a mix-up at an early-Egyptian boozing-ken. An extraordinary apparition, a fantastic faun of Aubrey Beardsley caught the roving riggish eye of the disguised Queen. She encouraged the

MARY GARDEN

advances of the anonymous animal. An Adonis à rebours. Pavley was this delicate monster and his subtle rhythms made Cléopâtre shiver. Here the music was too prudish.

Stravinsky or Richard Strauss would have given the screw an enharmonic wrench. Act III saw the Queen attired at once so sonorously and exquisitely that the vast audience gasped with admiration. It is, however, the tavern scene that will save the tawdry work. The anatomical wigwagging of the two golden lads set the lobby buzzing. Cléopâtre is doomed to packed houses in the future. Nothing succeeds like true spirituality.

Mary Garden is Cléopâtre, as she is Mélisande and Thaïs. It is not a rôle that taxes her dramatic resources or her personal pulchritude. All she did was to look beautiful and turn on the full voltage of her blandishments. Men went to the ground before that dynamic yet veiled glance, like soldiers facing a machine-gun. It is uncanny, the emotion she projects across the footlights and with such simple but cerebral means.

That she would have been burned at the stake a few centuries ago, this lovely witch, is no conjecture. Her nose is not "tip-tilted like the petal of a flower," as Cléopâtre's is said to have been; nevertheless, she is the tawny Egyptian. And she has never spoken so eloquently as in this parlando part. Perhaps the most poignant criticism was carelessly uttered by a big policeman who had strayed in during the garden scene. "Some Queen!" he said. And the definitive words had been spoken. Fie on naughty professional opinion after that memorial phrase!

MÉLISANDE

Once upon a time we called this "precious" lyric work Wagner and Absinthe, for there are many rumors of Tristan and Isolde in it, and the opalescent music, drugged with dreams, has the numbing effect of that "green fairy" no longer permitted in la belle France. Like all epigrams, this is only a half-truth. In the Belgian poet's The Death of Tintagiles—so wonderfully interpreted in tone by Charles Martin Loeffler—his marionettes are beginning to modulate into flesh and blood, and, like the mermaid of the fairy story, the transformation is a painful one. We note the achievement of a new manner in Pelléas and Mélisande. Played in English first by Forbes-Robertson and Mrs. Patrick Campbell, the piece created a mixed impression in London, though it may be confessed that, despite the scenic splendor, the acting transposed to a lower realistic key this lovely drama of souls. No play of Maeterlinck's is so saturated with poesy, replete with romance. There are episodes almost as intense as the second act of Tristan. We listen for King Mark's distant, tremulous hunting-horns in the forest scene when Pelléas and Mélisande uncover their hearts.

From a photograph copyrighted by Davis and Eickemeyer

MARY GARDEN AS MELISANDE

MARY GARDEN

The second act begins at an immemorial fountain in the royal park. Here the young Prince sits with the wife of his brother. Mélisande is the most convincing full-length portrait of the poet. Exquisitely girlish, she charms with her strange Undine airs. Mélisande is enveloped in the haze of the romantically remote. At times she seems to melt into the green tapestry of the forest. She is a woodland creature. More melancholy than Miranda, she is not without traces of her high-bred temperament; less real than Juliet, she is also passion-smitten. You recall Melusina and Rautendelein. Not altogether comprehensible, Mélisande piques us by her waywardness, her fascinating if infantile change of moods. At the spring the two converse of the water and its healing powers. "You would say that my hands were sick today," she murmurs as she dips her fingers into the pool. The dialogue is as elliptical as if written by Browning or Henry James. But the symbol floats like a flag.

The mad apostrophe to the hair of Mélisande is in key with this moving tableau. Perhaps Maeterlinck took a hint from the mournful tale of his friend, the Belgian poet Georges Rodenbach (Bruges-la-Morte), with its reincarnation of a dead woman in the form and features of a live one. The beautiful hair of the new love serves but to strangle her. Pelléas is more tender.

"I have never, never seen such hair as thine,

Mélisande. I see the sky no longer through thy locks. . . . They are alive like birds in my hands." The last scene, as Mélisande dies of a broken heart, even when read on the printed page, is pity-breeding. It is the tragedy of souls distraught. "She must not be disturbed," urges the venerable Arkel. "The human soul is very silent. . . . The human soul likes to depart alone. . . . It suffers so timorously. . . . But the sadness, Golaud, the sadness of all we see. . . . 'Twas a little being so quiet, so fearful, and so silent. 'Twas a poor little mysterious being like everybody." Pascal comes to the mind here. No matter the splendor of human lives, we must die alone.

The speech of the poet in its rhapsodic rush merges into Debussy's music. That we shall ever see another such ensemble as at the Manhattan Opera House years ago is doubtful. Mary Garden is Mélisande. No further praise is needful. All her trumpery rôles, Thaïs, Gismonda, Cléopâtre, with their insincere music and pasteboard pathos, are quickly dismissed. Her Mélisande is unforgettable.

MONNA VANNA

This opera was first heard here on February 17, 1914, at the Metropolitan Opera House, with Mary Garden, Vanni Marcoux, and Huberdeau. It had been produced by the Boston Opera Company in December, 1913, and by the

MARY GARDEN

present organization January 23, 1918. Miss Garden was the heroine on that occasion, and was greeted with overwhelming applause. The première of the play Monna Vanna occurred at the Nouveau Théâtre, Paris, May 17, 1902. We had the good fortune to see it a week later. Georgette Leblanc was the original Monna. Jean Froment, Darmont, and Lugné Poé were the other principals. The drama enjoyed an immediate success all over Europe from Bergen to Palermo. London alone stood firm against its blandishments. The censor forbade a production. New York first saw it in English with Bertha Kalich at the old Standard Theatre, Harrison Gray Fiske, manager.

As a play it was a new departure for Maeterlinck. It is almost theatric. In the heyday of his glory Sardou never devised anything more arresting than the dénouement—setting aside consideration of the psychologic imbroglio. There are spots in the dramatic scheme which tax the credulity. However, something of the improbable must always be granted a playwright, be he never so logical. The rapid mental change of Vanna hints at a native-born casuist, an Italian Renaissance type of mind. Her love of Colonna could not have been deep-rooted. But she did not betray him in the tent, and yet she has been adjudged profoundly immoral; in a word, not to put an edge too fine upon the sophistries of the situation, this heroine committed an imaginative infidelity as well as uttering a splendid falsehood. The madness of the finale is the logical outcome of her passion for Prinzevalle. All that has gone before in her life had been a bad dream. The true, the beautiful moment is at hand. It will be both her revenge and justification.

She goes to Prinzevalle in his cell. "This must end here; it is too perfect. . . . It is one blaze about me and within me. . . . Oh, some death will run its sudden finger round this spark and sever us from the rest!" Thus Browning sings In a Balcony.

The play's the thing! though it did not seem to catch the conscience of the composer. Nevertheless, Monna Vanna is more grateful to our ears than Gismonda. There are too many "things" that are set to music in the Sardou libretto, while Maeterlinck deals only with the primal passions—love, jealousy, hatred, conflict of wills. There is more unity in action and mood in the older score. The music is Wagnerian from first to final curtain, but it is cleverly assimilated and swifter, more poignant. The introduction to the third act recalls the third act of Valkyrs; so we were not surprised to find Brunhilde pleading, or to hear the chorus shrilly cry out the Valkyr theme. In the tent scene, Tristan and Isolde reign, as might be expected. The first act has been cut and to its advantage.

At our first view of Mary Garden as the mediæval Judith who fetches to Pisa her beloved Holofernes, we frankly confess that the impres-

From a photograph copyrighted by Mishkin

MARY GARDEN AS MONNA VANNA

MARY GARDEN

sions of her interpretation were strong. Monna Vanna will rank in her portrait-gallery among the finest. It far outshines Gismonda, as Monna herself outshines the incredible, erotic Duchess of Athens. There was no attempt to make a disrobing scandal in the tent scene, which would be obviously theatrical flimflam. Miss Garden disposed of the situation simply. She did not appear half-nude, but clothed in exquisitely-toned draperies. But if she did not show her lovely person, she spilled for us the soul of the heroine who saved her country and lost her reputation. In the opening act she did little, but suggested the psychology of a woman who had begun to loathe a supine husband. Note the nuance with which she uttered "J'rai, mon père," and the repetition when she says it to Colonna. It was like molten steel at first; it was cold, rigid steel, the steel of unalterable resolution the second time. Yet how tender is her "Si" when she turns to her fuming spouse.

There was tenderness in the tent scene, yes, true tenderness, not expressed by the sentimental symbols of the English theatre, but in the restrained terms of the French tradition; therefore, more eloquent, more artistic, despair and pride modulating into amazed joyfulness at meeting her early friend, stern Prinzevalle. But the last scene gave us the most moving side of this wonderful woman's art. The shock of incredulity caused by her husband's suspicions, merging into the supreme ecstasy as she grasps the key that is to unlock the future—in sooth, no such acting has been witnessed for a long time. The scale was essentially smaller than Bernhardt's, but as subtle as the art of Sarah were the indications of love triumphant with death staring her in the face. The tiny play of shadows round her eyes and mouth as she sees her lover trapped were touching. That she was a picture in every act is a matter of course. Her slow steps to the open door most impressive. It was a veritable march to the scaffold. Fevrier's music in this last episode rings true.

GISMONDA

Of Mary Garden it is always the correct thing to say that she is charming. True. Charming, and also many other qualities she boasts. She is exquisite, and she is sometimes a great dramatic artist. But her voice is a sonorous mirage. The lower register is still rich, sombre in coloring, thrilling when she wills. The gift of temperamental ecstasy is hers, though the character she paints so subtly is hardly worth the powder and shot to blow it sky-high. A sensual prowling panther, notwithstanding the al fresco exhibition of mother-love in Act I.

The panther glides from its midnight jungle to meet its mate, and then Miss Garden's magic begins to operate. Her soliloquy is the finest bit of psychology expressed in voice, mimique, and with the entire arsenal of her personal

MARY GARDEN

beauty that we have seen on any stage, dramatic or lyric, for years. She needs an intimate atmosphere. Her diction, her phrasing, her general grasp of the rôle are most impressive. She has distinction in every pose, distinction in the carriage of her head and arch of the neck.

Her cadenced step in the first scene is replaced by rhythmic movements in the second act that reveal her glowing inner life. She is all flame and gold—except when she sings above the staff. Even then she infuses it with a characteristic timbre. A singing-actress. People like Mary Garden because she has that rarest of artistic virtues—personality.

THAÏS

During the first week of last season's Chicago opera the temperament of Mary Garden was carefully chained in its cage; nevertheless, we overheard its growls in Gismonda, but the mock-Fafner at the bottom of the cistern outroared Miss Garden's tame panther. In Monna Vanna there were whimperings and menacing claws. The feline had no chance to spring, not even in the tent scene. At a matinée in the Lexington Theatre Thaïs was sung by the Chicago Opera Association, and now or never! we said, the temperament so artistically expressed, rather canalized and exquisitely distributed, in the two other operas, will leap. It did. In the palace of Thaïs the panther appeared for a few moments—and

BEDOUINS

it assumed the form of hysteria. The famous courtesan of Alexandria experienced a true "conversion," the physical manifestations of which were well-nigh pathological. "You have created a new shudder," wrote Victor Hugo to Charles Baudelaire after the production of his Flowers of Evil. The "nouveau frisson" of Miss Garden is thrilling, and must have appalled the well-meaning, stupid Athanael.

This singing-actress does not widely depart from her usual interpretation, except that slight perpetual novelty which we expect from her. Her last scene is beautiful in conception and execution; the "spiritual" flirtation on the mossy bank as piously piquant as ever. The kiss suggested and evaded set us to wondering again at the morose monk. In the early acts Thaïs is too restless. The firm yet plastic lines of the character are thereby disturbed. She looked lovelier than ever, and she did not sing in the best of voice. A trying week was behind her; besides, the domesticated panther must have tugged hard and frequently at its leash.

CARMEN

I attended Miss Garden's reading of the score for my first time, and freely admit my mixed feelings. We were assured by perfectly honorable lobbyists that the last season the Garden version was much better, more temperamental; and one who had overheard her in

MARY GARDEN

Paris swore that she was a seething caldron in Act II. Her interpretation seems to us to be "overpainted," to employ studio argot. Like the canvas in Balzac's Unknown Masterpiece, there is little left of the original design, except perhaps a miraculously painted foot.

There were bits here and there that are admirable; the slow awakening of her interest in the toreador as he thunders forth that supreme song of table d'hôtes. We see some delicate and definitive notations, yet it is lost in the cloudy chaos of the scene. All the strong theatrical points are deliberately renounced; the first tumultuous entrance, the Habanera, Seguidilla, and the duo in Act II. The renunciation suggests technical heroism, but it doesn't help us much in the development of the character.

Her Carmen is essentially frigid. And it is neither sinister nor sensuous. To be sure, it is different, but then so is Hedda Gabler "different." We went to see, to hear, Carmen, and Hedda—in a lyric mood—was more often adumbrated than the Mérimée-Bizet gypsy. The disturbing element of the performance was the undeniable fact that, granted her idea of the rôle, she didn't even "get it across." She missed fire in Act III, in the card episode particularly. Nor did she look bewitching. We quite understand her avoidance of the conventional posing, hipping, strutting, and inane postures; yet there should have been compensations. (In the days of Calvé the criticism was "Elle se hanche trop.")

BEDOUINS

These were slim, not her singing, nor yet the beautiful shawl that might have been designed by Sorolla y Bastida. The famous fan we missed. If Mary Garden had but lavished a tithe of her blandishments on her Don José that she so recklessly, so alluringly bestowed upon Marc-Antoine Maguenat in Cléopâtre, we might have been won over a little to her general conception. This Carmen was a distinguished dame. Lilli Lehmann alone outshone her in aristocratic Sevillian courtesy. But Lilli could sing. And Lilli had not the Aberdeen-cum Philadelphia-cum Chicago-cum Boston complex of Mary.

We have since learned that the singer was grievously indisposed. And she surely missed the Don José of Dalmores and Muratore.

And on this rather chilly note of dissent I prefer to end. Of Miss Garden's twenty or thirty other rôles it is hardly necessary to speak. Her Louise and Salome, so dissimilar, yet both incomparable, need no belated praise. She is unique. Thus endeth the Book of Mary the Garden.

V

MÉLISANDE AND DEBUSSY

GEORGE MOORE has remarked that we never speak of Shakespeare or Hugo or Flaubert as the authors of any particular work. Simply to utter their names suffices. I give the illustrations haphazard. Any great artist will do. From Claude Debussy we never ask of what he is the composer. Pelléas and Mélisande is his monument; rather, Mélisande and Pelléas; as, in the case of Isolde and Tristan, it is the woman who is protagonist. Is it because in creating characters of our mother's sex that the Eternal Masculine is projected across the feminine soul? Or, is woman the genuine, the aboriginal force, that we unwittingly obey, all the while calling her "little woman"? (condescendingly, of course). Oh, what a joke of almost cosmical proportions it would be if the latter supposition be the truer one! But mere male mortals may always console themselves with the ineluctable fact that it is man who has endowed woman with a vital figure in the arts. He has created Ophelia and Gretchen, Beatrice and Francesca, the Milo Venus, the Winged Victory and Isolde, Lady Macbeth and Emma Bovary, Carmen and Mélisande. Honors, then, are even. Even if models existed in nature, the art of man it was that shaped them and breathed life into their clay. But Mélisande is the protagonist in the drama.

The music to Maurice Maeterlinck's strangely haunting play is so wedded to the moods and situations that as absolute music it is unthinkable. And these moods are usually "con sordino." Despite his musicianship, Debussy is obviously a "literary" composer; his brain had first to be excited by a dramatic situation, a beautiful bouquet of verse, an episode in fiction, or the contemplation of a picture.

Why demand if the initial impulse be the Monna Lisa or a quatrain by Verlaine? A composer who can interpret in tone the recondite moods of Baudelaire, Verlaine, Mallarmé, or the dramatic prose-poem of Maeterlinck, need not have been daunted by criticism; in sooth, it is the angle of critical incidence that must be shifted to adapt itself to the new optique. Pelléas and Mélisande is a study in musical decomposition; the phrase is decomposed, rhythms are dislocated, the harmonic structure melts and resolves itself into air. His themes are developed in opposition to the old laws of musical syntax. But what have laws in common with genius? Once assimilated, they may be broken as were broken the stone tablets by the mighty iconoclast, Moses. Besides, every law has its holiday. In the Debussyan idiom there seems to be no normal sequence. I say seems, for much water has gone under the bridge since his appearance,

MÉLISANDE AND DEBUSSY

and compared with Schoenberg, Stravinsky, Ornstein, and Prokofieff he is a conservative; in another decade he may be called a reactionary. Life is brief and art is swift.

Our ears were not accustomed to his novel progressions and the forced marriage of harmonies. His tonalities are vague, but his values just. The introduction to the forest scene when Golaud discovers Mélisande is of an acid sweetness. Without anxious preoccupation Debussy has caught the exact Maeterlinckian note. As it is impossible to divorce music and text—Debussy seems to be Maeterlinck's musical other self—so it is needless to dwell upon the characteristic qualities of the score. It is like some antique and lovely tapestry that hypnotizes the gaze. It has the dream-drugged atmosphere of Edgar Allan Poe; the Poe of the dark tarn of Auber, of Ligeia, of Ellenora, of Berenice, and Helen, those frail apparitions from claustral solitudes and the Valley of the Many-Colored Grass, all as exotic as they are incorporeal. It is the complete envelopment of the poem by an atmospheric musical haze shot through with gleams of light never shown before on land or sea.

We pardon the monotone of mood and music, the occasional muffled cacophonies, the lack of exterior action, and the absence of climaxes; after so long waiting for a passionate outburst, when it does come it is overpowering in its intensity. In music the tact of omission has never been pushed so far. From the pianoforte partition little may be gleaned of its poetic fervor, its reticences, its delicate landscapes, psychologic subtleties. The pattern seldom obtrudes, as the web is spun "exceeding fine." The orchestration reveals the silver-greys of Claude Monet and the fire-tipped iridescence of Monticelli. His musical palette proclaims Debussy a symbolist, one in the key of Verlaine, who loved nuance for its own sake and detested flauntingly brilliant hues. "Pas la couleur, rien que la nuance . . . et tout le reste est littérature," sang Paul of the asymmetrical jaws and supernal thirst.

Debussy is the most interesting of contemporary music-makers and the most subtle composer for the pianoforte since Chopin. His originality is not profoundly rooted in the history of his art, but his individuality is indisputable. He is a musician doubled by a poet. He is almost as Gallic as Chopin is Polish. Debussy shows race. His artistic pedigree stems from a grafting of old French composers upon ultramodern methods. Wagner, Chopin, certain aspects of Liszt, and Moussorgsky. The visit he made to Russia in 1879 had important consequences. He read the manuscript score of Boris at Rome, he absorbed Moussorgsky and the whole-tone scale, and this influence contributed to the richness and complexity of his style. Above all, he is a stylist. He has Wagner at his finger-tips, and, like Charpentier, he can't keep Tristan out of his music; it is his

MÉLISANDE AND DEBUSSY

King Charles's head. Naturally such highly peptonized aural diet is not nourishing. Like the poetry and prose-poems of Stéphane Mallarmé, too much Debussy becomes trying to the nerves. Schumann has spoken of the singularly irritating effect of muted dissonances. Pelléas is nearly all muted. The mental and emotional concentration involved in the hearing of this music fatigues as does no other music; not even Tristan.

The range of ideas, like the dynamic range, is limited. Yet there is magic in his music, the magic of evocation. Not to describe, but to evoke, in effortless imagery, is the quintessence of his art. He is a painter of cameos and aquarelles. Never does he carve from the big block; an exquisite miniaturist, he does not handle a bold brush, nor boast the epical sweep of his predecessors; Berlioz for one. But he is more intimate, he is the poet of crepuscular moods. The sadness of tender, bruised souls is in his pages. Of virility there is little trace, it is music of the distaff, and seldom sounds the masculine ring of crossed swords. Chopin, too, had his nocturnal moments, but he also wrote the A flat Polonaise, with its heroic defiance of a Poland crushed yet never conquered; with its motto: "Jescze Polska nie zginiela!"

Long before his death this French master was critically ranged. Lawrence Gilman, the most sympathetic of his commentators, is also the fairest. To his essays I go for delectation. It would be rash to say that Debussy had achieved his artistic apogee; he may have had surprises in store, but it is safe to conclude that Pelléas and Mélisande is his masterpiece, that the dewy freshness of L'Après Midi d'un Faune would never have been recaptured. The symphonic suite, Printemps, the Nocturnes, La Mer, and Images, at once reveal the strength and limitations of Debussy, who was not a builder of the "lofty rhyme," though he is a creator of complex rhythms; not a cerebral composer—like Vincent d'Indy, for example—but an emotional one; not a master of linear design, but a colorist; a poet, not an architect. His vision is authentic. He knew that the core of reality is poetry; he lived not at the circumference but the hub of things. He loathed the academic. He is the antipodes of Saint-Saëns. He gave us a novel nuance in music, as did Maeterlinck in literature. (Think of Interior with its motive —again Poe—the fear of fear!) Debussy is a composer of nuance, of half-hinted murmurings of "the silent thunder afloat in the leaves," of the rutilant faun with his metaphysical xenomania, of music overheard, and of mirrored dreams. Little wonder he sought to interpret in his weaving tones Baudelaire and Verlaine, Mallarmé and Maeterlinck. He was affiliated to that choir of sensitive and unhappy souls, of which Maurice Maeterlinck is the solitary survivor. A poet himself, Claude Achille Debussy, even if he had never written a bar of music.

MÉLISANDE AND DEBUSSY

One summer evening in 1903 I was introduced to him at a café on the Boulevard des Italiens. Debussy spoke a few polite words when I told him that I belonged to the critical chain-gang. He had written much musical criticism, chiefly memorable for its unsympathetic attitude toward Schubert and Wagner, not because of reasons chauvinistic, but doubtless the result of a natural reaction against the principal educative forces in his life. At least once in his career an artist curses his artistic progenitors. Wagner must have hated Weber because of his borrowings from him, and I am quite sure Chopin despised Hummel; internal evidence may be collated in the Pole's wide departure from the academic patterns of Hummel's passage-work. However, Debussy never went so far as his friend Jean Marnold, who in the Mercure de France concludes a comparative study of Pelléas and Tristan in these words: "Le pathos de Tristan vient trop tard; si tard, qu'il semble aujourd'hui, à sa place adéquate en notre Opéra toulousain." Yet if Tristan came so late, how is it that there is so much of its music in Pelléas? a fact that Philip Hale doubts. There's the score. Who steals my idea steals trash; 'tis something, nothing; 'twas mine, 'tis his, and has been slave to thousands; but he that filches from me my style robs me of that which not enriches him and makes me poor indeed! (This is reorchestrated to suit the simile.) Tristan always seems to be waiting in the wings when Pelléas is played, awaiting his cue to enter. It never fails to be given by Debussy.

Later I asked Maurice Maeterlinck his opinion of Debussy's music to Pelléas and Mélisande. It was an imprudent question, for Lucienne Bréval had captured the rôle of Mélisande, not Georgette Leblanc. Maeterlinck is a polite man, and his answer was guarded; nevertheless, his dislike of the music pierced his phrases. To him it was evident that his play needed no tonal embellishment, that it was more poetic, more dramatic, without the Debussy frame. He is quite right. And yet the spiritual collaboration of poet and musician is irresistible. And in the garden of the gods there is only one Mélisande. Some little dramas, like little books, have their destiny. The composer of Pelléas and Mélisande suffered from the nostalgia of the ideal, suffered from homesickness for his patrie psychique, the land of fantasy and evanescent visions. The world will not willingly forget him.

VI

THE ARTISTIC TEMPERAMENT

It was twenty minutes to Eternity on a sunny morning in Gotham. The breakfast room was large, airy, and the view of upper Manhattan from the various windows gave one a joyous sense of our quotidian life, its variety and spaciousness. Central Park, a square of dazzling emerald, the erect golden synagogue on the avenue, the silver hubs of the wheels on passing carriages across the East Drive, were pictures for eyes properly attuned. The four eyes, however, in this particular apartment, were busily engaged in devouring, not the dainty breakfast spread before them—eyes eat, too—but the morning newspapers. On the walls were framed photographs. She as Juliet. He as Tristan. She as Isolde. He as Faust. She, Carmen. He, Siegfried. A versatile pair. Theirs had been a marriage prompted by love. A magnificent, a devastating passion had amalgamated their destinies—Paul Bourget would have said "sublimes." They still loved despite the poignant promiscuity of matrimony, although married nearly a year. They also loved others. And in the morning hours they hated one another with the holy hatred engendered by perfect sympathy. And they were so consumedly happy that they couldn't stay indoors for a day. It is easy to love fervidly; it is hard to hate intelligently. On one point, however, this wonderful soprano and glorious tenor were united —they despised musical criticism, even when it was unfavorable. Banishing Mildred, the pretty English maid—she was too pretty about six in the evening, so He noticed—to the bedroom, they read the newspapers undisturbed. They read aloud, and occasionally as a duet. She freely embroidered her commentaries. He embellished his with indignant outbursts.

"Dearest, hear this. What a beautiful notice from Spoggs. I appreciate it all the more because he was once épris of that Garden woman. I honestly believe the man is truly in love with me." "Pooh! Sweetheart, a music-critic has only ink and ice-water in his veins. Spoggs is in love with his hifalutin' phrases. All the rest is cannonading canaries. If he saw you in the right key he would never speak of your second-act Isolde. That's just where you fall down, darling. Whereas my third-act Tristan—" "Dear old boy. How you do run on. Always jealous when his poor little wifie is praised." "I jealous? Of—you!" Longa pausa! Suddenly she exclaims: "Oh, you poor man! Did you read what he said of your make-up last night? I hate that man now. He is so unjust—to you; though he does admire me. Why, what's the

THE ARTISTIC TEMPERAMENT

matter, baby? Where are you going? Your coffee is cold—" He storms out of the room, stumbling over Mildred on her knees near the door, either praying or polishing the keyhole with her lustrous eyelashes. Familiarity may breed contempt, but contiguity breeds, tout simple.

It really happened. In this instance I have transposed the key to opera. The true story deals with a well-known actress and her first husband, also her leading man. Two prima donnas under one roof. She read him to his death with unfavorable criticisms. I know of a more curious case. He was an idealist of an idealism so lofty that he often stumbled over the stars, enmeshed himself in constellations and took the sun for footstool. Her eyes, young as yesterday, were like an Irish sea-green mountain lake; at dusk, a sombre pool, profound at dawn as a sun-misted emerald. He painted. She sang. He painted her portrait. Then he painted other women's portraits. Each portrait he painted was the portrait of his wife. She was beautiful. At first society was amused, flattered, and finally resented the unsought compliment. Time drove the enamored couple asunder. They were too happy. She married again, happily. He remarried. I saw the last portrait he had painted of his second wife, a lovely creature. As in a pictorial palimpsest the features of his first wife showed in the new text; the expression of her eyes peeped through the other woman's eyes. A veritable obsession this, comparable to the exquisite and melancholy tale of Georges Rodenbach and the dear dead woman of Bruges-la-Morte.

What is the artistic temperament—so-called? Years ago I wrote to great lengths of "The Artist and His Wife," quoting ancient saws and modern instances to fatten my argument that artistic people are, in private life, very much like others; if anything, more human. I proved, by a string of names beginning with the Robert Brownings and the Robert Schumanns, that artists may marry or mix without fear of sudden death, cross words, bad cookery, rocky behavior, or diminution of their artistic powers. "There are no women of genius," said that cross-patch celibate, Edmond de Goncourt; "the only women of genius are men." A half-truth and a whole lie. Artistic men are as "catty" as the "cattiest" women. But why dwell only upon the incompatibility of artists? Doesn't Mr. Worldly Wiseman sometimes weary of his stout spouse? Why does the iceman in the adjacent alley beat the skinny mother of his children? Or why does a woman who never heard of Nora Helmer, Hedda Gabler, or Anna Karenina leave her husband, her family, not for the love of a cheap histrion, but because she thinks she can achieve fame as a "movie" actress? Is it not the call of the exotic, the far-away and unfamiliar? A woman can't live alone on stone without the bread of life at intervals. The echoes of

THE ARTISTIC TEMPERAMENT

wanderlust are heard in the houses of bankers, tailors, policemen, politicians, as well as in the studies of artists, poets, and musicians.

But the artist's misdemeanors get into print first. The news is published early and often. A beautiful young actress, or a rising young portrait-painter, a gifted composer, talented sculptor, rare poet, brilliant pianist, versatile writer—when one of these strays across the barrier into debatable territory, the watchmen on the moral towers lustily beat their warning gongs. It is prime matter for headlines. To the winds strong lungs bawl the naked facts. Depend upon it—no matter who escapes the public hue and cry, the artist is always found out and his peccadilloes proclaimed from pulpits or yawped over the roofs of the world. Why, you ask, should a devotee of æsthetic beauty ever allow his feet to lead him astray? Here comes in your much-vaunted, too-much-discussed artistic temperament—odious phrase! Hawked about the market-place, instead of reposing in the holy of holies, this temperament has become a byword and a stench in the nostrils. Every coney-catcher, prizefighter, or cocotte takes refuge behind "art." It is become a name accursed. When the tripesellers of literature wish to rivet public attention upon their wares, they cry aloud: "Lo, the artistic temperament!" If an unfortunate woman is arrested she is usually described in the police-blotter as an "actress." If a fellow and his wife tire of too much bliss, their "temperaments" are aired in the courts. Worse—"affinities" are dragged in. Decent folk shudder and your genuine artist does not boast of his "artistic temperament." It has become gutter-slang. It is a synonym for rotten "nerves."

A true artist abhors the ascription of temperament, keeping within the sanctuary of his soul the ideal that is the mainspring of his creation. The true artist temperament is, in reality, the perception and appreciation of beauty, whether in pigment, form, tone, words, nature, or in the loftier region of moral rectitude. It may exist coevally with a strong religious sense. And it may be gayly pagan. But always for the serious artist the human body is the temple of the Holy Ghost, as Mother Church, profoundest of psychologists, has taught. The dignity of men and women dare be violated only at the peril of their immortal souls. The artistic temperament adds new values to every-day life and character. But its possessor must not parade this personal quality as an excuse for self-indulgence. That he leaves to the third-rate artisan, to the charlatan, to the buffoon who grins through a horse collar, to the vicious who shield their vileness behind a torrid temperament. Now, art and sex are correlated. Sex is the salt of life. Art without sex is flavorless, hardly art at all, a frozen simulacrum. All great artists are virile. And their greatness consists in the victory over their temperaments; not in the triumph of mind

THE ARTISTIC TEMPERAMENT

over matter—futile phrase—but in a synthesis, the harmonious comminglement of intellect and artistic material. Sensualist your artist may be, but if he is naught else, then his technical virtuosity avails him not. He cannot achieve artistic grandeur. The noblest art is the triumph of imagination over temperament.

Too often a rainbow mirage is this entering into wedlock of two congenial souls.

When He whispers—it is the marrying month of June and the moon swims above in the tender blue—"Why, dear, it is just as easy for two to live as one on fifty dollars a week," the recording angel smiles, then weeps. Nor has the hardy young adventurer spiders on his ceiling. He dares to be a fool, and that is the first step in the path of wisdom. But She? Oh, She is enraptured. Naturally they will economize; occasional descents into cheap Bohemias; sawdust, pink wine, pinker wit, pinkest women. No new gowns. No balls. No theatres. No operas. No society. It is only to be Art, Art, Art! So they bundle their incompatible temperaments before an official and are made one. At least they are legally hitched. She plays the piano. He paints. A wonderful vista, hazy with dreams, spreads before them. She will teach a few pupils, keep up her practice, and save enough to study some day with a pupil of a pupil of Leschetizky. He will manfully paint, yes, a few portraits, though landscape is his ambition. But it is hard to resist the bribes of our dear common life. They try, they fail.

A year passes. What a difference! Gone are the dreams. There are many spiders on the ceiling now. To pay for the food they eat, to own the roof over their heads, are their ultimate desires. She looks paler. He may or may not drink; it doesn't much matter. There are no portraits painted; an artist must be doubled by a society man to capture commissions, to enjoy the velvet vulgarities of the new-rich. And artists demand too much of their wives. She must be a social success; also a combination of cook and concubine. Women are versatile. Women are born actresses. It was a woman, not a man, who discovered the art of leading a double life on ten dollars a week. But on thrice that amount they can't run a household, watch the baby—oh, wretched intruder!—play like Fannie Bloomfield Zeisler, and look like an houri. To be a steam-heated American beauty, your father must be a billionaire.

The artist-woman is a finely attuned fiddle. You may mend a fiddle, but not a bell, says Ibsen. True, but if you smash your fiddle the music is mute. And every day of fault-finding snaps a string, or reduces its tautness. How long does beauty endure? Begin misunderstandings. Pity, the most subtly cruel of the Seven Deadly Virtues, stalks the studio. Secretly She pities him. Secretly He pities her. Pity breeds hatred. Difference develops dis-

THE ARTISTIC TEMPERAMENT

content. At breakfast, the most trying time of the twenty-four hours—oh, the temperamental breakfasts when we were young and delightfully miserable!—even when you haven't anything to eat—at breakfast, He pities her flushed face as She runs in from the kitchen with eggs and coffee. No longer is She a sylph in his eyes. The fifty dollars a week seem shrunken, not enough for one to live upon, much less two or three. She pities him because He is flushed from his night's outing. His appetite, like his temper, is capricious. In her eyes He is the ordinary male brute (feed the brute!). Then He becomes imprudent and flings Schopenhauer at her head. That old humbug of a misogynist, who was always elbow-deep in woman scrapes! But She has no time to retort with Ibsen and Shaw for his swift discomfiture. The milkman is dunning her, and as baby must have pure milk She smiles at her foolish young man and teases him for the money. He looks blankly at her as He dives into empty pockets. This sort of thing may last for years. In reckless despair He may throw his lamp at the moon, She her bonnet over the windmill. Female suffrage will make such conditions impossible in the future by forbidding men the ballot. Like a sensible shoemaker let him stick to his last, or, to shift the image, let him grind the handle of the domestic barrel-organ while She collects the coppers.

It is when the lean years are upon the philandering artist, the years of thin thoughts and bleak regrets, that he may miss the loving wives of his past. Then will he cry in the stillness of his heart: O Time! Eternal shearer of souls, spare me thy slow clippings. Shear me in haste, shear me closely! You see, he remains the literary artist, and in the face of death he wears his shop mask. His artistic affinity, encountered late in their earthly pilgrimage, congratulates herself that her latter lonesome years won't be burdened by the ills and whims and senile vanity of an old man. She may be a spinster and boast the artistic temperament. Or she may escape that fate by marrying a sensible business or professional man, who pays the freight and admires her pasty painting, her facile, empty music-making, her unplayed plays, unread verse and novels—that are privately printed. Thus doth Nature hit the happy mean. He who could hold hands with a pretty girl in eleven languages consoles himself with his corroded memories. After all, has he not been a success, has he not eluded entangling matrimonial alliances? Ah, the artistic temperament!

During a certain London silly season some enterprising imbecile posed this query: Can a woman on the boards remain virtuous? This absurd question set Great Britain buzzing. His Grace the Archbishop answered, and every Tom, Dick, and Harry rushed into type to record their precious opinions. The theatrical profes-

THE ARTISTIC TEMPERAMENT

sion rose as a single woman. Mrs. Kendal and Mary Anderson were held up as shining patterns, which they are. But there were many sceptics. George Moore's Mummer Worship was hurled at the camp of the optimists. Rachel, Sarah Bernhardt, and Duse were adduced by the pessimists. Finally it occurred to the one intelligent person in all London to interview George Bernard Shaw.

"Mr. Shaw, do you think a woman can be virtuous in the theatre?"

"Why should she be?" asked St. George, and then and there the moral symposium went up in a burst of uncontrolled laughter. Mr. Shaw is like the little candid girl in the crowd; for him the truth is always naked. So is the artistic temperament.

VII
THE PASSING OF OCTAVE MIRBEAU

OCTAVE MIRBEAU was a prodigious penman. When Remy de Gourmont called Paul Adam "a magnificent spectacle" he might have said with equal propriety the same of Mirbeau. A spectacle and a stirring one it is to watch the workings of a powerful, tumultuous brain such as Mirbeau's. He was a tempestuous force. His energy electric. He could have repeated the exclamation of Anacharsis Clootz: "I belong to the party of indignation!" His whole life Mirbeau was in a ferment of indignation over the injustice of life, of literature, of art. His friends say that he was not a revolutionist born; nevertheless, he ever seemed in a pugnacious mood, whether attacking society, the Government, the Institutes, the theatre, the army or religion. There is no doubt that certain temperaments are uneasy if not in opposition to existing institutions, and while his sincerity was indisputable—an imperious sincerity, a sincerity that was perilously nigh an obsession—Mirbeau seemed possessed by the mania of contradiction. After his affiliations with Jules Vallès and the anarchistic group he was nicknamed "Mira-

THE PASSING OF OCTAVE MIRBEAU

beau," and, indeed, there was in him much of the fiery and disputatious, though he never in oratory recalled the mighty revolutionist. Nevertheless, he was a prodigious penman.

He was born in Normandy, 1850 (Ernest Gaubert says 1848), the country of those two giants, Gustave Flaubert and Barbey d'Aurevilly. He died early in 1917. His Odyssey, apart from his writings, was not an exciting one. Well born and well educated, he took a violent dislike to his clerical instructors, and as may be noted in Sébastien Roch (1890), he suffered from the result of a shock to his sensibilities because of an outrageous occurrence in the course of his school years. He early went to Paris, like many another ambitious young man, and began as an art-critic, but his first article on Monet, Manet, and Cézanne was also his last in the journal *l'Ordre;* it created so much scandal by its attack on those mud-gods of art, Meissonier, Cabanel, Lefebvre and Bouguereau, that he was drafted into the dramatic department. There he did not last long. After a violent diatribe against the House of Molière he found himself with several duels on his hands and enjoyed the distinction of a personal reply from Coquelin. He wrote for a little review *Les Grimaces*, and in 1891 defended Jean Grave's La Société Mourante and composed a preface for that literary firebrand. He had dipped into the equivocal swamp of politics and had been a sous-préfet (at St. Girons, 1877), but the experience did not lend enchantment to his patriotism. He saw the inner machinery of a democracy greasy with corruption and it served him as material for his political polemics.

His first decade in Paris he wrote for such publications as *Chroniques Parisiennes*, *La France*, *Gaulois*, and *Figaro*. The entire gamut of criticism was achieved by him. He was fearless. His pen was vitriolic and also a sledgehammer. Like old Dr. Johnson, if his weapon missed fire he brained his adversary with its butt-end. A formidable antagonist, yet the obverse of his medal shows us a poet of abnormal sensibilities, a loather of all injustice, a Quixote tilting at genuine giants, not missing windmills; also a man of great literary endowment and achievement. His critics speak of a period of discouragement during which he smoked opium, though without ill consequences. His was not a passive temperament to endure inaction. Like others, he had perversely imitated Baudelaire and De Quincey, but soon gave up the attempt. A nature trembling on the verge of lytic pantheism and truculent satire, Mirbeau had a hard row to hoe, and it is gratifying to learn that as he conquered in his art so he conquered himself. He waged war against Octave Mirbeau to the last. And no wonder. He has written stories that would bring a crimson blush to the brow of Satan.

Turning the pages of the principal Paris reviews to which he copiously contributed we find

THE PASSING OF OCTAVE MIRBEAU

him calling the financial press blackmailers; the law reporters "vermine judiciaire"; French journalism decidedly decadent: "The press kills literature, art, patriotism; it aggrandizes the shop and develops the shopkeeping spirit. It exalts the mediocre painters, sculptors, writers. Its criticism is venal." As for the theatre—from the frying-pan into the fire! The theatre is the prey of mediocrity, wherein Le Maître de Forges is pronounced a masterpiece!

The comedians ("les tripots revenus; cabotinisme") of La Comédie Française come in for their share. Emile Zola, naturally enough, has his allegiance, but he dealt hard raps on the skulls of his followers, the Zolaettes, who hung on the fringe of the novelist's dressing-gown. He admired Barbey d'Aurevilly and Elémir Bourges, as well he might; he attacked Daudet, Paul Bourget, Ohnet, Legouvé, Feuillet, Sarcey —dear old Uncle Sarcey, how Huysmans and Mirbeau did pound him!—and, last and worst, the art-critic of the *Figaro*, Albert Wolff. But he deserved the flaying.

In *La Presse* Mirbeau saluted the genius of Rodin, Maupassant, and praised Paul Hervieu. He adored Victor Hugo, not only as supreme poet but as humanitarian—the very quality that to-day so many find monotonous in his lyrics. But there was more than a strain of humanitarianism in Mirbeau. He was truly a Brother to Man, but he never exploited it as do sentimental socialists. It was the spectacle of poverty, of the cruelty of man to man, of the cruelty to animals—he wrote a novel about a dog—that set the blood boiling in his veins and forced him to utter terrible, regrettable phrases. His friends grieved, yet the spectacle was not unlike a volcano in action. That all this was prejudicial to the serenity of his art is not to be doubted. Mirbeau cared little. Let art perish if he accomplished a reform! Yet he has written some almost perfect pages, and in the presence of nature his angry soul was soothed, ennobled. A poet was slain in him before his vision became voice. He loved the figure of Christ and he drifted into the mystic and lovable theories of Kropotkine, Elisée Reclus, and Tolstoy. Their influence is manifested in his Lettres de ma Chaumière (1886). These tales overflow with sympathy and indignation. The French peasant as he is, neither idealized by Millet nor caricatured by Zola, is painted here with an intimate brush—it is painted miasma, one is tempted to add. That he was an unyielding Dreyfusard is a matter of history.

It may be said in passing that Mirbeau had not the stuff in him to make a sound or satisfactory critic of the Fine Arts. He was too one-sided in his Salons, his enthusiasms were often ill-placed, and he resembled Zola in his vocabulary of abuse if any one disagreed with him. M. Durand-Ruel, where he was liked for his sterling qualities, has a pamphlet of Mirbeau's on the Impressionists. Published here it would

THE PASSING OF OCTAVE MIRBEAU

have resulted either in a libel suit or a prosecution for obscenity. His definition of a certain art-critic is unprintable. When he hated he stopped short of nothing. A true Celt. But how he could tune down the peg of the false heroic to make sound the mean music of mean souls! There are a dozen men in Paris who were riddled by his shot and shell. He did not spare the Government and told some wholesome truths about the Tonkin affair. But he was not all fire and fury. He had intellectual charity, and the artist in him often prevailed. He was destructive, and he could be constructive. He could be charming and tender, too, and his style ranged from thunder-words to supple-sweet magic.

The constructive in him was artistic, but when the propagandist reins were between his teeth his judgments were muddied by his turbulence. And how clearly he could judge was proved by his clairvoyant article in *Le Figaro* on an unknown Belgian, by name Maurice Maeterlinck (1890). Mirbeau literally discovered Maeterlinck; and while we now smile over the title of "Belgian Shakespeare," there is no denying the flair of the Parisian critic. Certainly he made a better guess than the amusing Max Nordau, who once described the author of The Treasures of the Humble as "a pitiable mental cripple." In 1888 L'Abbé Jules appeared. It was Mirbeau's first novel. For the chief character he went to his uncle, a priest of rather singular traits. The book became a burning scandal.

Le Calvaire (1887) confirmed the reputation of the young writer. He certainly had a predilection "pour la poésie de la pourriture," as one critic puts it. But Calvary is a masterpiece and his least offensive fiction. The story of the little soldier who shoots an Uhlan in the war of 1870 and then tries to revive the dead man, finally kissing him on the forehead as a testimony of his fraternal feeling, is touching. Sébastien Roch, the third novel, is full of verity and power only marred by a page, one of the most hideous in French fiction (irrespective of avowedly crapulous stories). But Mirbeau has testified to its truth elsewhere. The hero becomes a victim to aboulia, or the malady of doubt. Happiness is not for him and he dies in the Franco-Prussian conflict. Le Jardin des Supplices (1899) set Paris cynically shivering with a new sensation. This garden of tortures is the most damnably cruel book in contemporary fiction. It was conceived by a Torquemada of sadism. Yet Mirbeau disclaimed any notion of writing for mere notoriety. These sombre pages of blood and obscenity were printed to show the cruelty and injustice of all Governments. The Chinese were selected as masters of the most exquisite tortures. A vile nightmare is the result. It demands strong nerves to read it once through; a rereading

THE PASSING OF OCTAVE MIRBEAU

would seem incredible. Swift is in comparison an ironical comedian.

Les Mémoires d'une Femme de Chambre (1901) is backstairs gossip, though the purpose is not missing; again satire of the better classes, so-called. Les vingt-et-un jours d'un Neurasthénique (1902) need not detain us, nor such one-act pieces as Vieux Ménage (1901), Amanto (1901), Scrupules (1902), or Le Foyer, with Natanson (1908). He also wrote a preface to Margaret Andoux's story, Marie Claire. The first important dramatic work of Mirbeau was Les Mauvais Bergers, in five acts, produced at the Théâtre de la Renaissance (December 14, 1897). We can still evoke the image of Sarah Bernhardt in the last act, an act charged with pity and irony. The play, because of its political and social currents, created a dolorous and profound impression. The work has in it something of both The Conquest of Bread and The Weavers. In Les Affaires sont les Affaires, produced at the Théâtre Français (April 20, 1903), Mirbeau is at his satirical best. The play has been shown here, but in a colorless, unconvincing style. In De Feraudy's hands the character of Isidore Lechat, both a type and an individual —one of our modern captains of industry (in the old days, a chevalier of industry?)—was perfectly exhibited. After witnessing in June of the same year a performance of this bitterly satirical comedy I met the author, who appeared as mild-mannered a pirate as ever cut a poet or scuttled a ship of State.

Paul Hervieu told me at the time that the bark of this old growling mastiff was worse than his bite; but his victims did not believe this. He was, in his dynamic prime, the best-hated publicist in all Paris—and that is saying a lot, for there were also Barbey d'Aurevilly, Ernst Hello, Louis Veuillot, J. K. Huysmans and several other virtuosi in the noble art of making foes. Decidedly, Mirbeau was not a lagger behind those pamphleteers and dealers in corrosive verbal values.

That he could be human was shown in his vertiginous automobile story La 628-E8, where, after retelling what Victor Hugo had hinted at in his Choses vues, Mirbeau made an apology to the daughter—or was it granddaughter?—of Mme. Hanska Balzac for a certain chapter which relates the Russian lady's doings on the heels of her great husband's death. Mirbeau was not legally compelled to withdraw this chapter, as it was a thrice-told tale in Paris, but a friend explained to him the lady's distress and he promptly made the only amend he could. This man had also a prodigious heart.

VIII
ANARCHS AND ECSTASY

LEST we forget. While competition is the life of cocottes, the rival opera companies that fill the air of Gotham with their lyric cries offer to the truly musical only the choice between two despairs; with our accustomed happy indecision we prefer Leopold Godowsky to Puccini. We frankly confess our love of symphonic music, and would rather listen to a Beethoven string quartet played by the Flonzaleys than all the operas ever written; the majority of them depicting soul-states in a sanatorium. However, there is the charm of aversion, and that piques the curious. Music in opera is prodigal, never generous. It is the too-much that appalls. It is as reticent as a female politician and a hundredfold more attractive. Flying fish, these singing-actors. They needs must swim and fly. Winged fish, birds with fins. It is an ambiguous art, the operatic, and it is devised to tickle the ears, dazzle the eyes, of the unmusical and myopic. It breeds personal gossip, never thought. For God's sake, let us sit upon the ground and tell sad stories of Mary Garden's celebrated eyebrows! (This modern instance, for Mary always goes first, as Henry

BEDOUINS

Arthur of the Jones family would say, does not necessitate Shakespearean quotation marks.)

From Bach to Scriabin, have not all composers been anarchs? At first blush the plodding John Sebastian Bach of the Ill-Tempered Clavichord seems a dubious figure with which to drape the red flag of revolt. He grew a forest of children. He taught early and late. He played the organ in church of Sundays. Nevertheless, his music proves him a revolutionist. And, like any good social democrat, he quarrelled with his surroundings. He even went out for a drink during a prosy sermon—all sermons are necessarily prosy, else they wouldn't be sermons—and was almost discharged by his superiors for returning late; a perpetual warning to thirsty organists. If Lombroso had been cognizant of this suspicious fact he would have built a terrific structure of degeneration theories with all sorts of inferential subcellars. Stranger still, the music of Bach remains as revolutionary as the hour it was written. No latter-day composer has gone so far as some of his fantasies. Mozart and Gluck depended too much on aristocratic patronage to play the rôles of anarchs; yet tales are extant of their refusal to lick the boots of the mighty or curve the spine of the suppliant. Handel! A fighter, a revolutionist born, a hater of tyrants. And the most virile among musicians except the peasant Beethoven—since the recent war become a Belgian composer! His contempt for rank and its entailed snobberies was like a

ANARCHS AND ECSTASY

blow from a muscular fist. Haydn need not be considered. He was a henpecked Croatian, and strange stories are related of this merry little blade, truly a chamber-music husband. Mendelssohn was Bach watered down for general consumption. Schubert and Schumann were anarchs, but the supreme anarch of art was Beethoven, who translated into daily practice the radicalism of his music.

Because of its opportunities for the expansion of the soul, music has ever attracted the strong free sons of the earth. It is, par excellence, the art masculine. The profoundest truths, the most blasphemous ideas, may be incorporated within the walls of a symphony, and the police none the wiser. Think of Chopin and Tchaikovsky and the arrant doctrines they preached. It is its freedom from the meddlesome hand of the censor that has made of music a playground for brave hearts. In his Siegfried and under the long nose of royalty Richard Wagner preached anarchy, put into tone, words, gestures, attitudes, lath, plaster, paint, and canvas, pronouncements so terrible that the Old Man of the Mountain, as Bernard Shaw calls Government, if it but knew, would forbid his music, not because it was penned by a German, but because it is inimical to tyranny, therefore the most democratic music ever composed.

Chopin presents us with a psychic "equivalent of war," as William James has put it, in portions of his music, notably the polonaises;

BEDOUINS

while Richard Strauss has buried more bombs in his work than ever Chopin with his cannon smothered in roses, or Bakounine and his nihilistic prose. Liszt, midway in his mortal life, was bitten by the socialistic theories of Saint-Simon, and, though a silken courtier, he was an innovator in his music. Brahms was a free-thinker and a democrat, but closely hugged the classic line and seldom strayed from the boundaries of his Romantic park. Berlioz, Hector of the Flaming Locks, was, his life long, a fiery individualist. He would have made a picturesque figure waving a blood-red flag on the barricades. His fantastic symphony is charged with the tonal commandments of anarchy. Richard Wagner may not have shouldered a musket during the Dresden uprising of 1849, yet he was, with Roeckel and Bakounine, one of its inspirers. Luckily for us he ran away, else Tristan might have remained in the womb of eternal silence. Wagner may be called the Joseph Proudhon among composers; his music is anarchy incarnate, passionately deliberate, like the sad and logical music we find in the great Frenchman's Philosophy of Misery (by the way, a subtitle). His very scheme of harmonization is the symbol of a soul insurgent in the music of Richard Strauss. And what shall we say to the exquisite anarchy of Debussy and Ravel? To the cerebral insurrection of Schoenberg? To the devastating sirocco blasts of Scriabin, Stravinsky, Ornstein, and Prokofieff? The Neo-

ANARCHS AND ECSTASY

Scythians, who, like their savage forebears, throw across their saddle-bow the helpless diatonic and chromatic scales and bear away their prisoners to their ultimate goal; the unknown land of the sinister duodecuple scale! Ah! we did not heed years ago the wise words of our critical Nestor, H. E. Krehbiel, when he said, "'Ware the Muscovite!" (He denies having used this precise phrase. Too late. We have pinned it to paper and it will go marching down the corridor of destiny wearing his label.) Ecce Cossakus! Bad Latin, but reality. The Tartars are coming. Anarchs all.

And ecstasy! It is not an eminently modern quality in the Seven Arts. Sculpture did for a time resist the universal disintegration, this imbroglio of all the arts. Before Rodin no sculptor had so greatly dared to break the line, had dared to shiver the syntax of stone. Sculpture is a static, not a dynamic, art; therefore, let us observe the rules, preserve the chill spirit of the cemetery! What Mallarmé attempted in poetry Rodin accomplished in clay. His marbles do not represent, but present emotion, are the evocation of emotion; as in music, form and substance coalesce. If he does not, as did Mallarmé, arouse "the silent thunder afloat in the leaves," he summons from the vasty deep the spirits of beauty, love, hate, pain, joy, sin, ecstasy, above all, ecstasy. The primal and danger-breeding gift of ecstasy is bestowed upon few. Keats had it, and Shelley; despite his passion, Byron missed it, as did the austere Wordsworth—who had, perhaps, loftier compensations. Swinburne had it from the first. Not Tennyson and Browning only in occasional exaltation. Like the "cold devils" of Félicien Rops, coiled in frozen ecstasy, the winds of hell booming about them, the poetry of Charles Baudelaire is ecstatic. Poe and Heine knew ecstasy, and Liszt too; but Wagner, ill-tempered like all martyrs, was the master adept of his century. Tchaikovsky closely follows him, and in the tiny piano pieces of Chopin ecstasy is pinioned in a few bars, the soul rapt to heaven in a phrase. Richard Strauss has shown us a variation on the theme: voluptuousness troubled by pain, the soul tortured by the very ecstasy of ecstasy. Like Yeats, he is "Master of the Still Stars and of the Flaming Door." William Blake and his figures rushing down the secret pathway of the mystic, which zigzags from the Fourth Dimension to the bottomless pit of materialism, was a creator of the darker nuances of pain and ecstasy. A sadistic strain in all this.

Scriabin is of this tormented choir; as Arthur B. Davies, our own mystic, primitive painter. And Charles Martin Loeffler. It may be the decadence, as any art is in decadence which stakes the parts against the whole. That ecstasy may be aroused by pictures of love and death, as in the cases of Poe and Baudelaire, Wagner and Strauss, should not, therefore, be

From a photograph copyrighted by Matzene

MARY GARDEN AS SALOME

ANARCHS AND ECSTASY

adjudged morbid. In the Far East they hypnotize neophytes with a bit of broken mirror, for in the kingdom of art, as in heaven, there are many mansions. It was possibly a relic of his early admiration for the Baudelaire poems that set Wagner to extorting ecstasy from his orchestra by images of love and death, though doubtless the temperament which seeks assuagement in such a comminglement—a temperament more often encountered in mediæval art than now—was natural to Wagner. He makes his Isolde sing madly and mournfully over a corpse, and, throwing herself upon the dead Tristan, she dissolves into the ecstasies of sweet, cruel love; in Salome, Richard Strauss closely patterns after Wagner; there is the head of a dead man—though on a charger—and there follows a poignant ecstasy not to be found in all music. Both men play with similar counters: love and death, and death and love. In Pisa may be seen (attributed by Vasari) Orcagna's fresco, The Triumph of Death. It has been set to grotesque music by Liszt in his Dance of Death. Let us not forget the great Italian, Gabriele d'Annunzio, whose magnificent prose, from The Triumph of Death to Forsé Che Si, Forsé Che No, is a pæan to the tutelar gods of humanity, love and death. The sting of the flesh and the way of all flesh are intermingled in Rodin's astounding fugue, The Gate of Hell. First things and Last things, love and life, bit-

BEDOUINS

terness and death, have ever ruled the arts; and all great art is anarchic, cosmos and chaos cunningly proportioned.

But between the sublime and the silly there is only a hair's breadth. If not guided by tact and vision, the ecstatic in art and literature may degenerate into the erotic, and from the erotic to the tommyrotic is only a step. All this tumultuous imagery, this rhapsody Hunekeresque, is prompted by a photograph of Mary Garden, whose enigmatic eyes collide with my gaze across the Time and Space of my writing-desk. Your memory is wooed by the golden trumpets of Byzance, and when Mary speaks she wears the sacred Zaïmph of Salammbo. Voltaire, in Candide, was wise when he advised us: "Il faut cultiver notre Jardin."

IX
PAINTED MUSIC

PAINTED music. The common identity of the Seven Arts was a master theory of Richard Wagner and a theory he endeavored his life long to put into practice. Walter Pater, in his essay on The School of Giorgione, has dwelt upon the same theme, declaring music the archetype of the arts. In his Essays Speculative, John Addington Symonds has said some pertinent things on the subject. Camille Mauclair, in Idées Vivantes, seriously proposed a scheme for the fusion of the arts. The fusion would be cerebral, as the actual mingling of sculpture, architecture, music, drama, acting, painting, and dancing could never evoke the sensation of unity. Not thus is synthesis to be attained. It must be the "idea" of the arts rather than their material blending. A pretty chimera! Yet one that has piqued the attention of artists for centuries. It was the half-crazy E. T. W. Hoffmann, composer, dramatist, painter, poet, stage manager, and a dozen other professions, including those of genius and drunkard, who set off a train of fireworks that dazzled the brains of Poe, Baudelaire, and the later symbolists.

BEDOUINS

Persons who hear painting, see music, touch poems, taste symphonies, and write perfumes are now classed by the psychical police as decadent, though such notions are as old as art and literature. In his L'Audition Colorée, Suarez de Mendoza has said that the sensation of color-hearing, the faculty of associating tones and colors, is often a consequence of an association of ideas established in youth. The colored vowels of Arthur Rimbaud, which should be taken as a poet's crazy prank; the elaborate treatises by René Ghil, which are terribly earnest; the casual remarks that one hears, such as "scarlet is like a trumpet blast"—it was scarlet to the young Mozart; certain pages of Huysmans and Mallarmé, all furnish examples of the curious muddling of the five senses and the mixing of artistic genres. Naturally, this confusion has invaded criticism, which, limited in imagery, sometimes seeks to transpose the technical terms of one art to another.

Whistler, with his Nocturnes, Color-Notes, Symphonies in Rose and Silver, his Color-Sonatas, boldly annexed well-worn musical phrases that, in their new estate, took on fresher meanings, while remaining knee-deep in the swamp of the nebulous. Modern composers have retaliated. Musical Impressionism is enjoying its vogue and the New Poetry is desperately pictorial. Soul-landscapes and etched sonnets are titles not unpleasing to the ear. What if they do not mean much! There was a

PAINTED MUSIC

time when to say "she had a sweet voice" aroused a smile. What has sugar to do with sound? It may be erratic symbolism, this mélange of terminologies, yet, occasionally, it strikes sparks. There is a deeply rooted feeling that the arts have a common matrix, that, emotionally, they are akin. "Her slow smile" in fiction has had marked success, but when I wrote of the "slow Holland landscape," the phrase was suspiciously regarded. (I probably found it in Verlaine or Rodin.) The bravest critic of the arts was Huysmans, who pitched pell-mell into the hell-broth of his critiques any image that assaulted his fecund brain. He forces us to see his picture; for he was primarily concerned with the eye, not the ear. Flaubert represents in its highest estate a fusion of sound and sense and seeing; he was both an auditive and a visualist. His prose sings, while its imagery sharply impinges upon the optic nerve. Nor are taste and smell neglected—recall the very flavor of arsenic that killed Emma Bovary or the scents of the woodland where that adorable girl lingered with her lover. Joined to those evocations of the five senses there is a classic balance of sentence, phrase, paragraph, page; the syntactic architecture is magnificent, though not excelling the eloquent Bossuet or the pictorial Châteaubriand as to complex, harmonious structure. These three great French writers had polyphonic minds, and their books and the orations of the superb Bossuet englobe a world of ideas and sensations, music and painting.

And Botticelli? Was Botticelli a "comprehensive," as those with the sixth, or synthetic, sense have been named by Lombroso-Levi? Beginning as a goldsmith's apprentice (Botticello, the little bottle), Botticelli as a painter became the most original in all Italy. His canvases possess powers of evocation. He was a visionary, this Sandro Filipepi, pupil of the mercurial Fra Lippo Lippi and of the Brothers Poliajuolo, and his vision must have been something more than paint and pattern. A palimpsest may be discerned by the imaginative—rather let us say fanciful, since Coleridge set forth the categories—whose secrets are not to be easily deciphered, and are something more than those portrayed on the flat surfaces of his pictures. Like most artists of his period he painted the usual number of Madonnas; nevertheless, he did not convince his world, or succeeding generations, that his piety was orthodox. During his lifetime suspected of strange heresies, this annotator and illustrator of Dante, this disciple of Savonarola, is now definitely ranged as a spirit saturated with paganism, and yet a mystic. Does not the perverse clash in such a temperament produce exotic dissonances?

All Florence was a sounding-board of the arts when Botticelli paced its narrow streets and lived its splendid colored life. His sensitive nature absorbed, as does a sponge water, the

PAINTED MUSIC

impulses and motives of his contemporaries. The secrets lurking in the "new learning"—doctrines that made for damnation, such as the recrudescence of the mediæval conception of an angelic neuter host, neither for heaven nor hell, not on the side of Lucifer, nor yet with the starry hosts—were said to have been mirrored in his pictures. Its note is in Città di Vita, in the heresies of the Albigenses, and it may well go back to Origen. Those who could read his paintings—and there were clairvoyant theologians abroad in Florence—might make of them what they would. Painted music is less understandable than painted heresy. Matteo Palmieri is reported to have dragged Botticelli into dark corners of disbelief; there was in the Medicean days a cruel order of intelligence that delighted to toy with the vital faith and ideals of the young. A nature like Botticelli's, which frankly surrendered to new ideas if they but wore the mask of subtlety, was swept, no doubt, away in the eddying cross currents of Florentine intellectual movements. Mere instinct never moved him from his moral anchorage, for he was a sexless sort of man. Always the vision. He did not palter with the voluptuous frivolities of his fellow artists, yet his canvases are feverishly disquieting. The sting of the flesh is remote. Love is transfigured, though not spiritually, and not served to us as a barren parable, but made more intense by the breaking down of the thin partition between the sexes; a consuming emotion, not quite of this world nor of the next. However, the rebellion that stirred in the bosom of Botticelli never took on concrete aspects. His religious subjects are Hellenized, not after the sterner, more inflexible method of Mantegna, but resembling those of a philosophic Athenian who has read and comprehended Dante. His illustrations show us a different Dante, one who might not have altogether pleased that gloomy exile. The transpositions of the Divine Comedy by William Blake seem to sound the depths; Botticelli, notwithstanding the grace of his "baby Centaurs" and the wreathed car of Beatrice, is the profounder man of the pair.

His life, veiled toward the last, was not happy, although he was recognized as a great painter. Watteau concealed a cankering secret; so Botticelli. Melancholy is the base of the Florentine's work. As a young man he created in joy and freedom; but the wings of Dürer's Bat were outstretched over his brooding head. Melencolia! He could ask if there is anything sadder under the sun than a soul incapable of sadness. There is more poignant music in his Primavera, in the weary, indifferent countenances of his lean, neuropathic Madonnas—Pater calls them "peevish"—in his Venus at the Uffizi, than in the paintings of any other Renaissance artist. The veils are there, the consoling veils of an exquisite art, which are missing in the lacerated and realistic holy folk of the Flemish Primitives. Joyful-

PAINTED MUSIC

ness cannot be denied Botticelli; but it is not the golden joy of Giorgione; "Big George of Castelfranco." An emaciated music emanates from the eyes of that sad, restless Venus, to whom love has become a scourge of sense and spirit. Music? Yes, there is the "colored-hearing" of Mendoza. The canvases of Botticelli sound the opalescent overtones of an unearthly composition. Is this Spring, this tender, tremulous virgin, whose right hand, deprecatingly raised, signals as a conductor from invisible orchestra its rhythms? Hermes, supremely impassive, hand on thigh, plucks the fruit as the eternal trio of maidens with woven paces tread the measures of a dance we but overhear. Garlanded in blossoms, a glorious girl keeps time with the pulsing atmospheric moods; her gesture, surely a divine one, shows her casting flowers upon the richly embroidered floor of the earth. The light filters through the thick trees, its rifts as rigid as a candle. The nymph in the brake is threatening. Another epicene creature flies by her. Love shoots his bolt in mid-air. Is it from Paphos or Mitylene? What the fable? Music plucked down from vibrating skies, music made visible. A mere masque, laden with the prim, sweet allegories of the day, it is not. That blunt soul, Vasari, saw at best its surfaces. The poet Politian got closer to the core. Centuries later our perceptions sharpened by the stations traversed of sorrow and experience, lend to this immortal canvas a more sympathetic, less literal interpretation.

There is music, too, in the Anadyomene of the Uffizi. Still stranger music. Those sudden little waves that lap an immemorial strand; that shimmering shell, its fan-spokes converging to the parted feet of the goddess; her hieratic pose, its modesty symbolic, the hair that serpentines about her foam-born face, thin shoulders that slope into delicious arms; the Japanese group blowing tiny gem-like buds with their puffed-out cheeks; the rhythmic female on tiptoe offering her mantle to Venus; and enveloping all are vernal breezes, the wind that weeps in little corners, unseen, yet sensed, on every inch of the picture—what are these mundane things but the music of an art, original at its birth, and since never reborn? The larger, simpler, curved rhythms of the greater men, Michelangelo, Da Vinci, Shakespeare, Beethoven, are not in Botticelli. Nevertheless, his voice is irresistible.

Modern as is his spirit, as modern as Watteau, Chopin, or Shelley, he is no less ethereal; ethereal and also realistic. We can trace his artistic ancestry; but what he became no man could have predicted. Technically, as one critic has written, "he was the first to understand the charm of silhouettes, the first to linger in expressing the joining of the arm and body, the flexibility of the hips, the roundness of the shoulder, the elegance of the leg, the little shadow that marks the springing of the neck, and, above all, the carving of the hand; but even more, he understood "le prestige insolent des grands yeux."

Pater found his color cold and cadaverous, "and yet the more you come to understand what imaginative coloring really is, that all color is no mere delightful quality of natural things, but a spirit upon them by which they become expressive to the spirit, the better you like this peculiar quality of color." Bernard Berenson goes further. To him the entire canvas, Venus Rising from the Sea, presents us with the quintessence of all that is pleasurable to our imagination of touch and movement. . . . The vivid appeal to our tactile sense, the life-communicating motion is always there. And writing of the Pallas in the Pitti galleries, he most eloquently declares: "As to the hair— imagine shapes having the supreme life of line you may see in the contours of licking flames, and yet possessed of all the plasticity of something which caresses the hand that models it to its own desire!" And, after speaking of Botticelli's stimulating line, he continues: "Imagine an art made up entirely of these quintessences of movement-values and you will have something that holds the same relation to representation that music holds to speech—and this art exists and is called lineal decoration. In this art of arts Sandro Botticelli may have had rivals in Japan and elsewhere in the East, but in Europe never! . . . He is the greatest master of lineal design that Europe ever had."

Again, painted music; not the sounding symbolism of the emotions, but the abstract music of design. Nevertheless, the appeal of Botticelli is auditive. Other painters have spun more intricate, more beautiful webs; have made more sensuous color-music; but the subtle sarabands of Botticelli they have not composed. Here is a problem for the psychiatrist. In paint, manifestations of this order could be set down to mental lesion; that is how Maurice Spronck classifies the sensation. He studied it in the writings of the Goncourts and Flaubert. The giant of Croisset told the Goncourts that to him Salammbo was purple and L'Education Sentimentale grey, Carthage and Paris. A characteristic fancy. But why is it that scientific gentlemen, who predicate genius as eye-strain, do not reprove poets for their sensibility to the sound of words, to the shape and cadence of the phrase? It would appear that only prose-men are the culpable ones if they overhear the harping of invisible harps from Ibsen's Steeplejacks, or describe the color of the thoughts of Zarathustra. In reality, not one but thousands of people listen in the chill galleries of Florence to the sweet, nervous music of Botticelli. This testimony of the years is for the dissenters to explain. "Fantastico, Stravagante," as Vasari nicknamed Botticelli, has literally created an

PAINTED MUSIC

audience which learned to use its eyes as he did, fantastically and extravagantly.

He passed through the three stages dear to arbitrary criticism. Serene in his youthful years; troubled, voluptuous, and visionary during the Medicean period; sombre, mystic, a convert to Savonarola at the end. He traversed a great crisis not untouched. Certain political assassinations and the Pazzi conspiracy hurt him to the quick. He noted the turbulence of Rome and Florence, saw behind the gayly tinted arras of the Renaissance the sinister figures of supermen and criminals. He never married. When Tommaso Soderini begged him to take a wife he responded: "The other night I dreamed I was married. I awoke in such horror and chagrin that I could not fall asleep again. I arose and wandered about Florence like one possessed." Evidently not intended by nature to be husband or father. Like Watteau, like Baudelaire, like Nietzsche, grand visionaries abiding on the thither side of the facile joys of life, Botticelli was not tempted by the usual baits of happiness. His great Calumnia, in the Uffizi, might be construed as an image of the soul of Botticelli. Truth, naked and scorned—we see again the matchless silhouette of his Venus—misunderstood and calumniated, stands in the hall of a vast palace. She points to the heavens. She is a living interrogation-mark. Pilate's question? Botticelli was adored. But understood? An enigmatic malady ravaged his innermost being. He died poor, solitary, did this composer of luminous chants and pagan poems, this moulder of exotic dreams, and of angels who long for gods other than those of Good and Evil. You think of the mystic Joachim of Flora and his Third Kingdom; the Kingdom of the Holy Spirit which is to follow the Kingdom of the Father and the Kingdom of the Son; the same Joachim who declared that the true ascetic counts nothing of his own, save only his harp. "Qui vere monachus est nihil reputat esse suum nisi citharam." And you also recall St. Anselm, who said that he would rather go to hell sinless than be in heaven smudged by a single transgression.

A grievously wounded, timid soul, an intruder at the portals of Paradise, Botticelli had not the courage either to enter or withdraw. He experienced visions that rapt him into the ninth heaven, but when he reported them in the language of his design his harassed, divided spirit chilled the ardors of his art. In sooth, a spiritual dichotomy. And thus it is that the multitude does not worship at his shrine as at the shrine of Raphael. Do they unconsciously note the adumbration of a paganism long dead, but revived for a brief Botticellian hour? Venus or Madonna! Adonais or Christ! Under which god? The artist never frankly tells us. Legends are revived of fauns turned monks, of the gods in exile and at servile labor in a world that has forgotten them, but with a sublimated

PAINTED MUSIC

ecstasy not Heine's. When we stand before Botticelli and hear the pallid, muted music of his canvases we are certain that the last word concerning him shall not be uttered until his last line has vanished; even then his archaic harmonies may reverberate in the ears of mankind. But always music painted.

X

POE AND HIS POLISH CONTEMPORARY

IN the City of Boston, January 19, 1809, a son was born to David and Elizabeth Poe. On March 1, 1809, in the village of Zelazowa-Wola, twenty-eight English miles from Warsaw, in Poland, a son was born to Nicholas and Justina Chopin (Chopena or Szop). The American is known to the world as Edgar Allan Poe, the poet; the Pole as Frédéric François Chopin, the composer. On October 7, 1849, Edgar Poe died, poor and neglected, in Washington Hospital at Baltimore, and on October 17, 1849, Frédéric Chopin expired at Paris surrounded by loving friends, among whom were titled ladies. Turgenev has said there were at least one hundred princesses and countesses in whose arms the most wonderful among modern composers yielded up his soul. Poe and Chopin were contemporaries, and, curious coincidence, two supremely melancholy artists of the Beautiful lived and died almost synchronously.

My most enduring artistic passions are for the music of Chopin and the prose of Flaubert. In company with the cool, clear magic of a Jan Vermeer canvas, that of the Pole and French-

POE'S POLISH CONTEMPORARY

man grazes perfection. But as a lad Chopin quite flooded my emotional horizon. I had conceived a fantastic comparison between Poe and Chopin, and I confess I was slightly piqued when Ignace Jan Paderewski, not then Premier of Poland, assured me that Chopin was born in the year 1810, and not the year earlier. The date chiselled on Chopin's Paris tomb in Père Lachaise—a sad tribute to the mediocre art of Clésinger, who married Solange Sand—is, after all, the correct one, and this new date, which is also the old, is inscribed on the Chopin Memorial at Warsaw, Poland. I shall not attempt to dispute the claim; even the most painstaking of Chopin biographers, Prof. Frederick Niecks, admits his error. The latest biography, said to be definitive, by the Polish musicograph, Ferdinand Hoesick, I have not seen; the war impeded the translation. Yet I am fain to believe that too many parish registers were in existence, and perhaps the next one that is unearthed may give as new dates either 1808 or 1811. I prefer 1809, while apologizing for my obstinacy. Unhappily for future investigators, Russian Cossacks in 1915 ravaged with torch and sword the birthplace, not only destroying the Chopin monument, but burning his house and the parish church. These once highly esteemed vandals, pogrom heroes, and butchers of thousands of helpless Jewish women, children, and old men, only repeated at Zelazowa-Wola the actions of their forebears at Warsaw during the sanguinary uprising of 1831. The correspondence of Chopin, treasured by his sister, Louise Jedrzejewicza, and the piano of his youth were completely destroyed. (Louise died in 1855, and the other sister, Isabella Barcinska, in 1881.)

The love of Poe began early with me. My father had been a friend of the poet's in Philadelphia, and a member of the Poe circle during the forties of the last century; "roaring forties, indeed. That prime old comedian, Billy Burton, the ideal Falstaff of his day; John Sartain, the engraver, and father of William Sartain, the painter; Judge Conrad, who could move his listeners to tears when he recited the Lord's Prayer; the elder Booth, a noble tragedian much given to drink; Graham, the publisher, and several others whose names have escaped my memory, composed this interesting group. In his memoirs John Sartain has written of Poe and of a certain wild midnight walk in Fairmount Park. I remember the elder Sartain as an infrequent visitor at our house, and I also remember how I hung on his words when he spoke of Poe. My father told me that Poe would become a raving maniac after a thimbleful of brandy, so sensitive was his cerebral mechanism. But other authorities contradict this theory. Poe had been often seen to toss off a tumblerful of cognac neat. Last year at Atlantic City I met Mr. Hutzler, a well-known merchant of Baltimore, a spry young octo-

POE'S POLISH CONTEMPORARY

genarian and a seasoned raconteur. He told me, and in a vivid manner, of seeing Edgar Poe and Junius Brutus Booth hanging on to the same lamp-post, both helplessly drunk at midday. This happened about 1845, as the boys, Mr. Hutzler among the rest, trooped out to dinner from the public school on Holliday Street. Mr. Hutzler's memory has a mirror-like clearness, and he described the occurrence as if it had happened yesterday. Like irreverent schoolboys, they surrounded the greatest living Shakespearean actor and the greatest American poet and mocked at them.

We lived on North Seventh Street, and twice a day, on my trip to and from school, I passed the house where Poe had lived during his sojourn in Philadelphia, from 1838 to 1844. That house I should not have been able to locate to-day if my friend, Christopher Morley (charming writer, with a name that recalls spacious Elizabethan times: Kit Morley!), hadn't described it. This house, in which Poe wrote The Raven and The Gold Bug, is at the northwest corner of Seventh and Brandywine Streets. Another critic friend, Albert Mordell, assures me that the old pear-tree in the back yard still bears fruit for the present resident, Mrs. Owens. The house is the rear building of another numbered 530 North Seventh Street. Mr. Mordell sent me a photograph which shows a typical Philadelphia red brick structure with white shutters and marble steps. I have heard of many spots where Poe wrote The Raven, Fordham among the rest, but as boys we told ourselves when we stared at the old building: "Poe wrote his Raven and Gold Bug there!" It is something to remember in these piping times of hypocrisy and universal hatred of art, music, and literature.

It would be a strained parallel to compare Poe with Chopin at all points; nevertheless, chronological coincidences are not the only comparisons that might be instituted without exaggeration. True, the roots of Chopin's culture were more cosmopolitan, more richly nurtured than Poe's; the poet, like an air-plant, found his spiritual sustenance from sources unknown to the America of his day. Of Poe's intellectual ancestry, however, we may form some conception, though his learning was not profound, despite his copious quotations from half-forgotten and recondite authors, Glanvil, for example. Nevertheless, the matchless lines, "Helen, thy beauty is to me like those Nicéan barks of yore," . . . were struck off in the fire of a boyhood passion. Chopin had a careful training under the eye of his Polish teacher, Elsner; but who could have taught him how to compose his Opus 2, the Variations on Mozart's La ci darem la mano? Both Poe and Chopin were full-fledged artists from the beginning, their individualities and limitations sharply defined. Perhaps the most exquisite music penned by Poe is this same Helen, while the first mazourka of Chopin stamps him as an original poet. In the later productions of these men there is more than a savor of morbidity. Consider the Fantaisie-Polonaise, Opus 61, with its most musical, most melancholy cadences; or the F minor Mazourka, composed during the last illness of Chopin; a sick brain betrays itself in the rhythmic insistence of the theme, a soul-weary Wherefore? In the haunting repetitions and harmonies of Ulalume there is a poetic analogue. This poem, in which sense swoons into sound, possesses a richness of color and rhythmic accent that betoken the mentality of a poet whose brain is perilously unhinged. If alcohol produced this condition, then might a grateful world erect altars to such a wondrous god of evocation. Prohibition has not thus far produced a Poe. But he wasn't the creation of either alcohol or drugs, though they were contributory causes; they prodded his cortical cells into abnormal activity, made leap the neuronic filaments with surprising consequences. No, a profound cerebral lesion was the real reason why Poe resorted to brandy to soothe his exacerbated nerves, and not because he drank did he go to wrack and ruin. His "case" is like Baudelaire's and E. T. W. Hoffmann's; not to mention the names of James Clarence Mangan and Monticelli, one the singer of Dark Rosaleen, the other that master of gorgeous hues, fantasies of enchanted lands and crumbling linear designs.

Poe, then, like Chopin, did not die too soon.

BEDOUINS

Neurotic natures, they lived their lives with the intensity which Walter Pater has declared is the true existence. "To burn always with this hard, gem-like flame, to maintain this ecstasy, is success in life. Failure is to form habits." Alas! that way madness lies for the majority of mankind, notwithstanding the æsthetic exhortation of Pater. Poe and Chopin fulfilled the Pater conditions during their brief sojourn on our parent planet. They ever burned with the flame of genius, and that flame devoured them. They were not citizens of moral repute. Nor did they accumulate "mortal pelf." They failed to form habits, and while the psychic delicacy of Chopin proved a barrier against self-indulgence of the grosser sort, he contrived to outrage social and ethical canons even in tolerant Paris. The influence of George Sand, her ascendancy over his volition, worked evil and unhappiness. The delicate porcelain of his genius could not float down-stream in company with her brassy ware without ensuing disaster for the finer of the twain. Alcoholic neurosis did not trouble him, but he was tubercular, and that malady is more fatal than alcoholism. Poe was not precisely a drunkard; probably masked epilepsy accounts for his vagaries; such victims are periodical dipsomaniacs, "circulaires" is the term of the psychiatrists. His personality was winning, his speech electric, his eye alight with genius; but, then, the obverse of the medal! A sad, slouching creature, with

POE'S POLISH CONTEMPORARY

a cynic's sneer, a bitter tongue which lashed friend and foe alike, a gambler, a libertine—what has this unhappy poet not been called? Baudelaire asked whether the critical hyenas could not have been prevented from defacing the tomb of Poe. (He used Rabelaisian language in the original French.) Charles Baudelaire, a spiritual double of Poe, was another unhappy wraith of genius, and of the same choir of self-lacerated and damned souls.

Fancy Poe and Chopin in New York during the prosaic atmosphere of those days! If Chopin had not achieved artistic success at the Soirée of Prince Radziwill in Paris, 1831, he would probably have gone to America, where he might have met Poe. He had declared his intention to leave Paris for New York, and his passport was viséd "passing through." Poe and Chopin conversing! The idea is rather disquieting. Stendhal, not hoodwinked by Châteaubriand, with his purple phrases and poetic visions of virgin forests and sweet Indian girls in an impossible Louisiana, declared that America was materialistic beyond hope of redemption. Talleyrand knew better. However, it was better for the artistic development of the Polish composer that he remained in the Old World. Think of Chopin giving piano lessons to the daughters of the New-Rich at the fashionable Battery, and Poe encountering him at some conversazione—they had conversaziones then—and propounding to him Heine-like questions: Are the roses at home still in their flame-hued pride? Do the trees sing as beautifully as ever in the moonlight? Are humming-birds and star-dust—Francesca Astra—still as rare as ambergris? At a glance Poe and Chopin would have sympathized. In sensibility the American was not inferior to the Pole. Poe would have felt the "drummed tears" in the playing of Chopin, and in turn Chopin would not have failed to divine the vibrations of Poe's high-strung nature. Both men were mystics, were seers. What a meeting that would have been; yet inevitable misery might have come to the Pole in unsympathetic New York. A different tale if Poe had gone to Paris and enjoyed a meed of artistic success. Baudelaire, who was born in April, 1821, therefore a young chap in 1845, would have known him and, congenial souls, they would surely have gone to the devil quicker than apart. Baudelaire and Poe! There's a marvellous combination for you of fantasy, moonlight, rotten nerves, hasheesh, and alcohol! The fine flower of the genius of Poe might have bloomed more fragrantly on French soil; perhaps with the added note of depravity not in his sexless creations, and so corroding a note in Les Fleurs du Mal. Who may dare say! But then we might not have had the sinister melancholia, so sweetly despairing, so despairingly sweet, that we enjoy in the real Poe.

The culture of Chopin was not of a finer stamp than Poe's, nor was his range so wide. In their

POE'S POLISH CONTEMPORARY

intellectual sympathies both were rather narrow, though intense to an emotional poignancy, and both were remarkable in mood-versatility. Born aristocrats, purple raiment became them well. Both were sadly deficient in planturous humor and the Attic salt that conserves the self-mockery of Heine. Irony they possessed to a superlative degree. Both created rhythmic beauty, evoked the charm of evanescence. A crepuscular art; the notations of twilit souls and the "October of the sensations." Both were at their best in smaller artistic forms. When either one spreads his pinions for symphonic flight we think of Matthew Arnold's interpretation of Shelley: "beating in the void his luminous wings in vain." Which phrase truly is of Mat's own making, yet somehow misses the essential Shelley. Poe and Chopin supremely mastered their intellectual instruments. Artificers in precious cameos, they are of an artistic consanguinity because of their extraordinary absorption in the Beautiful. Poe wrote in English, but was he really as American as Hawthorne and Emerson were American? His verse and prose depict characters and landscapes that belong to No Man's Land, in that mystic region east of the sun, west of the moon. The American scene was unsympathetic to him, and he refused to become even morally acclimated. His Eldorado is "over the mountains of the moon, down the valley of the shadow." His creations are bodiless; shadow of shadows, the incarnation of Silence, set forth in spectral speech. Unlike any other native-born writer, he sounds better in a French garb; the Baudelaire translations improve his style, and Stéphane Mallarmé has accomplished an almost miraculous transposition of Ulalume. (The Raven—Le Corbeau—by the same master I do not care for as much, and with its refrain, "Jamais plus!" is not so musically sonorous as "Nevermore!")

Henry Beyle-Stendhal wrote in his witty, malicious manner that "Romanticism is the art of presenting to the people literary works which in the actual state of their habitudes and beliefs are capable of giving the greatest possible pleasure; Classicism, on the contrary, is the art of presenting literature which gave the greatest possible pleasure to their great-grandfathers." Stendhal is half right. A Classic is sometimes a dead Romantic. But Poe and Chopin remain invincibly Romantic, yet are Classics. Chopin is more human than Poe, inasmuch as he is patriotic. His polonaises are "cannons buried in flowers," his psychic bravery overflows in the Revolutionary Etude. He is Chopin. And he is also Poland. Like the national poet, Adam Mickiewicz, he struck many human chords, though some of his melodies could dwell in Poe's "misty mid-region of Weir," where Beauty boasts an icy reign. There is a disturbing dissonance in the Poe-Chopin case: Poe was a man without a country; Chopin had the priceless possession of Poland. On his heart was engraved "Poland." The love of Frédéric Chopin for his native land dowered him with a profounder nature than the Lucifer of American poetry, Edgar Allan Poe. But what enigmatic, beautiful souls!

XI
GEORGE LUKS

OF course, I knew in a vague way where Edgecombe Road and Jumel Place spotted the map, for I am a seasoned Manhattan cockney. But, after all, I mixed up the Jumel Mansion and the house of George Luks, and so I asked that painter for some travel indications. He sent me a map that was clarity itself. All I had to do was to sit in the Broadway subway till I reached One Hundred and Sixty-eighth Street; then take the elevator—as deep down in the bowels of the earth as if in the London Underground; on reaching the sidewalk proceed northward to One Hundred and Seventieth Street—the little arrows on the chart are marked; then eastward (another arrow) and behold! Amsterdam Avenue. There you enter a delicatessen bureau and tactfully inquire after Edgecombe Road.

I did all these things, and was recently told on a fine, breezy afternoon by a foreign youth that the road was in front of my face, as was Highbridge Park; around the corner was Jumel Place. Enfin! I said to the polite guide, and nosed my way till I saw an ideal cottage—though rather large for a cottage—with a big

GEORGE LUKS

studio window facing the north. Recalling what Luks had often said—"To hades with a north light; a man ought to be able to paint in a cellar!"—I wondered. Then I traversed a garden and broke into the house, a burglar, armed with a pen and a bagful of question-marks. It was the home of the only George Luks, who, happy boy, has a painting temperament with an "angel in the house" to protect him from the contact of a world of cruel critics, and is also the possessor of the disposition described as "bubbling." His favorite exclamation is: "Yours for happiness." He means it. It is the leading-motive of his life.

Here are domestic comfort, a north light, and plenty of models across the road in the open air, splashed by sunshine or shadowed by trees; babies, goats, nurse-girls, park loafers, policemen, lazy pedestrians, noisy boys, nice little girls with hoops, and the inevitable sparrows. Rocks are in abundance. The landscape "composes" itself. And you are not surprised, when ushered into the great studio on the second floor, to be confronted by canvases registering various phases of the vibrating world hard-by. Since he moved from down-town the painter is becoming more of a plein-airiste.

Luks doesn't wander afar for subjects. He still loves the familiar, the homely, the simple. It had been several years since I saw his work. Occasionally in Holland I would run across a canvas by Jan Steen, Adrien Brouwer, or even

BEDOUINS

Hals, that recalled Luks. His artistic affinities are Dutch rather than French; above all, he is an American painter to his blunt finger-tips. Beginning in the field of illustration, he was plunged up to his eyes in New York life. I believe it was Arthur Brisbane who first suggested to him that he should go in for painting in oils.

He went to Düsseldorf and survived that trying experience—a school that would submerge a Manet. Paris followed. But George is not a product of the schools. Theories sit lightly on his mercurial shoulders. He loathes "movements," and refers to the "new" men, cubists, lamp-post impressionists, and futurists in words that curdle the blood. Indeed, his vocabulary is as variegated and picturesque as his palette. As for the personality of the man—well, it is absolutely impossible to set down on paper any adequate description of him. He is Puck. He is Caliban. He is Falstaff. He is a tornado. He is sentimental. He can sigh like a lover, and curse like a trooper. Sometimes you wonder over his versatility; a character actor, a low comedian, even song-and-dance man, a poet, a profound sympathizer with human misery, and a human orchestra. The vitality of him!

Perhaps the simile of a man-orchestra is the most fitting. Did you ever see and hear those curious creatures, less rare in our streets a quarter of a century ago than now? I remember one in a small French city, a white-haired fellow who, with fife, cymbals, bells, concertinas

GEORGE LUKS

—he wore two strapped under either arm—at times fiddles, made epileptic music as he quivered and danced, wriggled and shook his skull. The big drum was fastened to his back, upon its top were cymbals. On his head he wore a pavilion hung with bells that pealed when he twisted his long skinny neck. He carried a weather-worn violin with a string or two missing; while a pipe that might have been a clarinet years before emitted but cackling tones from his thin lips. By some incomprehensible co-ordination of muscular movements he contrived simultaneously to sound his armory of instruments; and the whistling, screeching, scratching, drumming, wheezing, and tinkling of metal were appalling. But it was rhythmic, and at intervals the edge of a tune might be discerned sharply cutting through the dense cloud of vibrations, like the prow of a boat cleaving a fog. And the reverberating music swelled, multifarious and amazing, as if a military band, from piccolo to drum, were about to descend upon the town. A clatter and bang, a sweet droning and shrill scraping were heard, as the old chap alternately limped and danced in the middle of the roadway.

Now, George Luks is not venerable; he is a comparatively young man, yet he reminds me of that human orchestra. It is an image of lithe activity that he suggests. What has this to do with his art? Much. It is rhythmic, many-colored, intensely alive, charged with character and saturated with humanity, not forgetting humor. Pathos is not absent. In his latest productions I noted with satisfaction more repose, deeper feeling, more solicitude for his surfaces, the modulation of tones; and the same old riotous joy in color for color's sake. Yes, in his themes he still belongs to the illustrators. He seldom tells a definite story, but there is no mistaking his point of view.

I saw portraits of girls in masquerade that were expressed in terms of beautiful paint. A little red-head, the sheer tonal charm immediate, made me think of both Henner and Whistler. Then a Hals-like head, virile and sincere; a sensitively limned portrait of a young girl, his niece; a large canvas; charming girls under umbrageous trees, a veritable gamut of greens; an old woman who simply cried to be framed and exhibited—how many things did I not stare at, wondering over the inexhaustible fecundity, and groaning over the reckless prodigality, of this gifted man! With a tithe of his talent and personal quality other painters have achieved renown. However, he is not lacking in honors. He has plenty of admirers, plenty of commissions; yet do his friends wish that he would sometimes apply the brakes to that fiery temperament of his and steer his bark into less tumultuous waters. His art would gain thereby in finish, and distinction, and repose. And it might also die.

I once called George Luks "a hand and an eye." His power of observation is great. He

GEORGE LUKS

has the intensity of a Spaniard and the realism of a Dutchman. He is both exact and rebellious. Wherever he happens to pitch his tent becomes his studio; preferably in the open. But the East Side is his happy hunting-ground. In the Yiddish restaurants where old men with Biblical heads drink coffee and slowly converse; on Houston Street, when, apparently, the entire population is buying fish Shabbas-abend; in vile corners where the refuse of humanity drift, helpless, hopeless—there Luks catches some gleam of humor or pathos, some touch that Gorky-like brings before us in a dozen strokes of the brush or pencil a human trait which emerges to the surface of this vast boiling kettle like a spar thrown up by an angry sea. All happiness is not lost in those mean streets; a rift of wintry sunlight, a stray tune from some wheezy barrel-organ, and two children waltz with an unconscious zest of life that will survive until they are nonogenarians. Of such contrasts Luks is the master.

His Spielers is like a quivering page from— from whom? The East Side is yet to boast its Dickens. And Dickens would have enjoyed the picture of the little tousled Irish girl, with her red locks, who dances with the pretty flaxenhaired German child, surely a baker's daughter from Avenue B. Now, you might suppose that this vivid art, this painting which has caught and retained the primal jolt and rhythm of the sketch, must be necessarily rude and unscientific in technique. It is the reverse. This particular picture is full of delicious tonalities. The head of the blonde girl might be from an English eighteenth-century master, and the air—it fills the spaces with a fluid caress.

And his Little Gray Girl, a poor wisp of flesh wearing a grotesque shawl and hat, shivering in the chill of a gloomy evening, sounds touching music. The note of sentiment is not forced; indeed, the passages of paint first catch the eye, modulations of grays and blacks that tell of the artist's sensitive touch. He has wanton humors. He paints a French coachman, life-size, seated at a café table about to swill brandy. It is so real that you look another way. Or you are shown a collection of beggars who were famous a few years ago on Sixth Avenue, Broadway, the east side, Fulton Market: Matches Mary, the Duchess, the tottering Musician, the old Italian, "Gooda nighta, Boss!" and a host of nocturnal creatures since dead or in the hospital, perhaps in jail. Luks is their interpreter. Nor does he lean to the pessimistic; he is a believer in life and its characteristic beauty. The pretty he abhors.

There is the Duchess. In life she was an elderly hag with a distinguished bearing, a depraved woman of rank, who wore five or six dresses at once, on her head a shapeless yet attractive gear, and in her pocket she carried a fat roll of bills for purposes of dissipation, or bribery, or for bailing out some Tenderloin

GEORGE LUKS

wreck. She is maleficence incarnate. Just fancy this bird of the night set forth by a sympathetic brush, endowed with a life that overflows the canvas, and you see this grande dame strut by, the embodiment of evil, yet a duchess à la Sir Johsua, though à rebours. It is a sinister art which recalls the genius of Toulouse-Lautrec. With Lautrec the work of Luks has certain affinities. He may never have studied that painter; rather is it a temperamental resemblance, a certain tolerant way of seeing men and things. But Luks is not so cynical as the Frenchman.

And that striking embodiment of Whisky Bill, a once well-known personage in the American Parisian colony! Several judges have praised the Fraser portrait, which we greatly admire for its excellent qualities, but personally we plump for the head of Whisky Bill, the head of a great violinist and also a profound alcoholist. In Gorky's Nachtasyl there is an old actor who runs about the play exclaiming: "I have poisoned my organism with alcohol." We have never seen Whisky Bill, but we are sure from the canvas that he has poisoned his organism with alcohol. Nevertheless, a man who thinks, one who has suffered from the mirage of thirst, not one of the Hals or the Steen jovial drinkers. The spleen of life has killed the ideals of Bill. They are submerged in his melancholy eyes. As for his hair, we might almost compare it to Masson's engraving of the gray-haired man,

BEDOUINS

Guillaume de Brisacier, after Mignard; but with a difference—the hair is treated more luminously in mass than detail.

There are the usual number of studies from life, of Old Mary Curling Her Hair, a companion piece to the Goose Girl. The most characteristic picture in the Luks collection is an ideal head of Bobbie Burns's Suter Johnnie. Therein is the synthesis of all the more admirable qualities of Luks: humor, technical audacity, solid modelling, vital color, sweet sentiment, and a searching humanity, all of which combined make a vigorous appeal to the spectator. Luks sometimes plays to the gallery, but at the core he is sincere. His feet are set upon the mountain. He is not pausing to grasp at the flowers or the applause. But do not imagine because he is the smiling George Luks with the Napoleonic brow, round cherubic cheeks, and nimble wit, that he is easy to decipher.

As for The Pawnbroker's Daughter—she might have stepped out from some old Holland master's studio. The Dutch strain in Luks and his shrewd Yankee humor are here blended in the happiest manner. The girl is carrying a carafe on a tray. The rich comminglement of tones, the tribal "awareness" of the girl's glance, her tangled hair, and the smouldering splendor of her garb are indicated without a suspicion of bravura; yet one is conscious of virtuosity, clairvoyance, and sympathetic observation.

There is the reverse of the medal. No man

GEORGE LUKS

is made all of a piece, and the art of Luks has its seamy side. He displays an infernal impatience, that chief sin of heresiarchs, according to Cardinal Newman. He sometimes takes criticism in no amiable way. And the corollary of impatience is haste in execution. Luks seldom finishes a canvas. He must have five hundred stowed away in his studio. Many are not half-begun. Nevertheless, this rough handling of his material—neither irreverent nor careless—bears special fruits. Some subjects respond instantly to this treatment. Swift, brutal, seldom subtle, though suggestive, his portraits leap from the bare canvas into vital being. In the fury of his execution, when the fit is upon him he could cover miles of walls with figures. This itching of the nerves, this tugging of the muscles, which impels a pianist to play until Jericho falls or his listeners die, is but the special artistic organ of any artist keyed up to the pitch of intensity. Luks is the most normal man imaginable. Full of the kindly sap of life, he too often boasts his powers when he should be making lines and color patches. That is his very human side; "human—all too human"— as Nietzsche would say. Slightly inhuman is his capacity for sustained work—mind you, we don't say sustained in the sense of sticking at one picture until he has exhausted its possibilities, but a capacity for toil, prolonged, laborious.

This exuberance, this boiling over of energy, these dashes at reality, these slices of life, bold

BEDOUINS

portraits of men and women who dare to live, though only painted, this Human Comedy merely hinted at, are testimonies to the creative and tumultuous powers of a man who is of Rabelaisian energies. The saving fact is that Luks is not old, and knows what he most lacks. To advise him to paint like some one else, to make slim silk purses when he so superbly paints sows' ears, would be futile. He is not academic. He has a grim vein of irony that spells at a glance the tragi-comedy of life—his Parisian sketch-books would have attracted Daumier—and also a superabounding confidence that sometimes leads its owner into dubious, as well as devious, places.

But he is one of our native, commanding talents, and with study and experience must come the purging of the dross; with his mellowing Luks will take his proper place among his contemporaries, and it will be in the seats of the mighty—or nowhere. The only possible schooling that will hasten this result will be the stern self-schooling of George Luks. But he is just the style of man who may bid criticism go hang and nevertheless win out at the end. Like the turbulent and fleshly Bard of Camden, he can "sound his barbaric yawp over the roofs of the world," and make of this "yawp" an art extremely personal and arresting.

As a portraitist he has his good days and bad. When he is deeply gripped by his subject he is usually successful. The head of Senator Root

GEORGE LUKS

was criticised because of a certain hardness and rigidity in texture and pose, but there were critics who declared that the painter's psychology had revealed the essential Root—austere, profound, Machiavellian statesman and scholar. The self-portrait, like the Smoker of Brouwer, is the record of a passing mood. It is a swift sketch, and is Luks in the heydey of a happy, devil-may-care humor. Truly a ' human document.' I admire his landscape, Round Houses at High Bridge. The atmosphere is finely evoked; Luks knows his values. Steam, and again steam, is painted in a delicate scale of pearl-greys.

But even Lux pinxit becomes a long-drawn-out line of light. I bade my hosts good day. "I'll see you as far as the subway," said Luks. He accompanied me to the station, where you go down to the train in a lofty elevator, as you do in the gloomy London Underground. I had passed an admirable afternoon with a human painter. Some painters are not human.

XII

CONCERNING CALICO CATS

THIS is to be a sober Sunday sermon, even though it largely concerns Calico Cats. What is a calico cat? you will ask. The first we ever heard of the strange beast, after the Eugene Field poem, was at a concert of the Philharmonic Society, when Mortimer Wilson conducted a clever orchestral suite in which figured the Funeral of the Calico Cat; that is, a specific cat, one, let it be said in passing, that was quite tiny at the beginning of the music, but grew to monstrous proportions before its interment; a cat that would have put to blush the "Cheshire Puss" of Alice's in the fable. Cats in calico may be seen on the streets any Gotham summer day, but a calico cat—what in the world may that be? The simulacrum of a feline, an eidolon, such as Mr. Howell once described? We can't ask Mr. Wilson, because he might refer us to his charming score, which speaks for itself. Verhaeren, the Belgian poet, the greatest living poet at the time of his death at Rouen, with the solitary exception of Gabriele d'Annunzio, Emile Verhaeren has written about "Cats of ebony, Cats of flame," but, manifestly, a cat can't be both flaming and calico. We must turn to that

CONCERNING CALICO CATS

lover of cats, Charles Baudelaire, who wrote sonnets to his cats as others have penned praises of their mistresses' eyebrows. He discovered to France the genius of Richard Wagner and the genius of Edouard Manet, not to mention Poe's. Jules Claretie relates that Baudelaire said to him, with a grimace: "I love Wagner; but the music I prefer is that of a cat hung by his tail outside of a window, and trying to stick to the panes of glass with its claws. There is an odd grating on the glass which I find at the same time strange, irritating, and singularly harmonious."

Now, obviously, this is an invention. Perverse as Baudelaire undoubtedly was, he loved cats too much to torture them. Without knowing it, the late director of the Théâtre Français has described, "avant la lettre," as the etchers say, the music of the future: Schoenberg, Stravinsky, Ornstein, and Prokofieff. But calico cats! Not a spoor of them in all this, so we are forced to fall back upon symbolism, which seems to be the art of saying the reverse of what you think. (I nearly meant this.) In his Hunting of the Snark Lewis Carroll finds that it is a Boojum. Perhaps our calico cat is not a cat at all, but a critic. But then a cat may look at a critic, as a critic is privileged to stare a composer out of countenance. A calico cat may, for all we know, house the soul of a real cat. Therefore, children, do not treat it rudely! It may be watching you with its malignant, beady eyes, ready to spring, ready to scratch when you least expect it! And we should not forget Baudelaire, who would lower his voice when showing his friends some Polynesian idol of wood, bidding them not mock, because once upon a time a deity may have inhabited the rude carving. The remote ancestor of a calico doll may have been that scourge of a vanished geological epoch, the sabre-toothed tiger, just as the iridescent dragon-fly that flashes winged sunshine as it skims is the pitiful reduction of the dread Pterodactyl, the flying saurian, which also reappears as the Jabberwock (furnished with a monocle by Sir John Tenniel, ever a stickler for etiquette). The calico cat might be a prowling version of the Frumious Bandersnatch, with the claws that scratch.

But a truce to paleontology! Let us of the nonce assume that the cat in question stands for the tutelar totem of criticism. A mere figure of speech, "Hypocrite lecteur—mon semblable—mon frère!" I can see my surprised colleagues: He has called us musical lounge lizards, now we are calico cats! What the next recrudescence? In Hindu-land what Avatar? I remember the sage advice of Vance Thompson: When all trumps fail, write about your liver! He was speaking of criticism. Musical trumps are, as a rule, mesugah, in the classic parlance of pinochle; hence I fall back on a hypothetical hepatic condition, i. e., calico cats and criticism; criticism of music, art, literature, or mixed.

CONCERNING CALICO CATS

Swinburne's theory that "I have never been able to see what should attract a man to the profession of criticism but the noble art of praising" was vitiated in practice by the poet himself, who wrote scurrilously of any one who disagreed with him. "After all, what are critics?" asked Balzac, and later Disraeli-Beaconsfield. "Men who have failed in literature and art." Mascagni, the Single-Speech Hamilton of Italian composers, cried aloud in resentment that a critic was only a "compositore mancato." (Probably some fellow musician had wounded him with a pen.)

But every one is a critic, a calico cat, your gallery god, as well as the most stately practitioner of the gentlest art. The difference between your criticism and mine, as I have remarked elsewhere, is that I am paid for mine, and you must pay for your privilege to criticise. As some Paris wit said of a certain actress: "She is not beautiful, she is worse." A critic is never unjust—he is worse. Nevertheless, I prefer the plain critic's opinions rather than the professional pronouncement of a composer. He always knows more than the critic, yet I doubt his attitude, which is seldom disinterested. How could it be? Why should it be? Schumann, who "discovered" Chopin and Brahms, missed Wagner. In Wagner he met his critical Waterloo, and as George Moore wrote of Ruskin vs. Whistler: "It is the lot of critics to be remembered by what they have failed to understand."

Berlioz also missed Wagner—Wagner who had helped himself so generously to the ideas on instrumentation of the Frenchman. But Balzac did not miss Stendhal, whose generation refused to recognize his genius. The "creative" critics are few. Montaigne, Goethe, Sainte-Beuve, Taine, Baudelaire, Georg Brandes, Nietzsche, Pater, Benedetto Croce, Havelock Ellis, Matthew Arnold, Arthur Symons, Anatole France, De Gourmont, Edgar Saltus, Brownell—the list might be spun out, but these names suffice. Yet my idol among them, Sainte-Beuve, missed Balzac, Stendhal, Flaubert, and to Victor Hugo was inconsiderate—possibly on account of his affair with Adèle Hugo. Consider the Osrics of literature eternally embalmed in the amber of Sainte-Beuve's style, a fatal immortality for so many futile butterflies, and you will admit that he still lives when many a mighty reputation has withered.

In sheer wonderment George III asked how the apples got inside the dumpling. How can a critic criticise a creator! Oscar Wilde, shrewd enough when he so willed, has a middle term; critics who are "creative." But isn't he the man who looks on while the other fellow does things! He should be artist as to temperament, and he should have a credo. And like most prima donnas, he is "catty." He need not be a painter to write of painting, a composer to speak of music. His primary appeal is to the public. He is the interpreter. The psycho-

CONCERNING CALICO CATS

physiological processes need not concern us. There are the inevitable limitations. Describing music in terms of prose is hopeless. The only true criticism of music is the playing thereof. We are again confronted by the Vance Thompson crux: write about your liver, or the weather, or calico cats, as I am now doing. All the rest is technical camouflage. Of course, a catholic critic doesn't mean an unprejudiced one. A critic without prejudices would be a faultless monster, and like Aristides the Just, should be stoned.

Carl Van Vechten has told us of Erich Satie, the eccentric French composer, who sets snails and oysters to music, and, no doubt, has composed a Cooties Serenade for wind instruments with a fine-tooth comb obbligato, and we are amazed at the critical exposition of such a perplexing "case." To let his music speak for itself, would be unwise, as it is not sufficiently explicative. Rhizopods can't converse. Just here is where your music-critic, your calico cat, intervenes. After Van Vechten has polished off his man, we feel that we know all about Satie, so much so that we never wish to hear a bar of his crustacean music. The difference between tweedle-dum and tweedle-dee is infinitesimal, but that very difference may contain great art.

Professor, now Sir Walter Raleigh, has said that "Criticism, after all, is not to legislate but to raise the dead." Sometimes it raises hades. Millet declared that "there is no isolated truth";

BEDOUINS

Constable denied that a good thing is ever done twice, and Alfred Stevens—the Belgian painter, not the English sculptor—defined art as "nature seen through the prism of an emotion," thus forestalling the more pompous pronouncement of Zola in The Experimental Novel. These are not merely epigrams, but truths. On the other hand, recall what Velasquez is reported to have said to Salvator Rosa, according to Boschini and Carl Justi. Salvator had asked the incomparable Spaniard whether he did not believe Raphael to be the best of all the painters he had seen in Italy. Velasquez answered: "Raphael, to be plain with you, for I like to be candid and outspoken, does not please me at all." There were the mountains criticising, deep calling unto deep. All said and done, a question of temperament, this opinion of one great man about the work of another.

Therefore, brethren, it behooves us to be humble, as pride goeth before a fall. Like the industrious crow, the critic, or, as you will, the calico cat, should hop after the sowers of beauty, content to pick up in the furrowed field the grains dropped by genius. At best the critic sits down to a Barmecide's feast, to see, to smell, but not to taste the celestial manna vouchsafed by the gods. We are only contemporaries of genius, all of us, and the calico cat is the badge of our tribe. But who dares confess this shocking truth? And who shall bell the calico cat?

XIII
CHOPIN OR THE CIRCUS?

RATHER hotly I argued the question with my editor: "After all, music-critics are men and brethren," I said. "Except when they are sisters," he ironically interposed. I sternly resisted a temptation to blush and continued: "Because I love Chopin must I forever write of his music—toujours perdrix! It's an indigestion of strawberries, clotted cream, and green eyes. I'm suffering from spring-fever. Let me write a story about the circus." "Why not Ibsen?" interposed my editor, who is subtle or nothing. "He was a grand man," I assented, "but in the present case he is only red-herring across the trail. Suppose I mix up Chopin with sawdust merely for the sake of the mélange?" My chief assented, wearily. There are more important problems on the carpet than Chopin. Jim Beck vs. Pop Hylan in a catch-as-catch-can for the welter-weight championship. Or the celebrated Mrs. J. and the Beethoven-Hamburger steak controversy. Why not Chopin and sawdust? I retired with a thoughtful mien.

Had I ever been to the circus? What a singular question. Yet, yet—! No, I confessed to myself, I had not been to the circus for at

BEDOUINS

least three decades. Critics are tame cats away from their regular guests. In the concert-room or at the play, armed with our little hammers, we are as brave as plumbers; but on a roof garden, in church, at a circus, or innocently slumbering, we are the mildest gang of pirates that ever scuttled an American sonata or forced ambitious leading-ladies to walk the plank. We may go alone to the theatre with impunity and another fellow's girl, but at the circus we need a nurse to show us the ropes and keep us from falling under the elephants' hoofs. A private nurse—not necessarily old—say I, is the only safety for a critic out of his element; otherwise a sense of the dignity of our calling is not maintained.

Therefore, I swallowed my Chopin scheme without undue fervor and went to the circus. No matter which one. All circuses are in an attractive key to me. Thackeray said the same thing about the play, and said it better. Any circus will serve as a peg for my sawdust symbolism. Any Garden will do, so that it has a capitalized initial letter. (No allusion to Magical Mary.) The circus! What a corrective for the astringent Ibsen or the morbidezza of Sarmatia's sweet singer, Chopin! The circus. It is a revelation. One thing I regretted—that I could not be a boy again, with dirty hands, a shining brow, and a heart brimming over with joy. Peter Pan! Oh! to recapture that first careless rapture, as Browning or some other

CHOPIN OR THE CIRCUS?

writing Johnny said; surely he must have meant the circus, which is the one spot on our muddy planet where rapture rhymes with the sawdust ring.

"Have you ever seen Hedda Gabler?" I asked of the Finland giantess. We were wedged in front of the long platform at the Garden, upon which were the Missing Link, the Snake-Enchantress, the Lion-Faced Boy, the English Fat Girl—so fat—the Human Skeleton, the Welsh Giant, the Lilliputians, tattooed men, a man with an iron skull, dancers, jugglers, gun-spinners, "lady" musicians, and the three-legged boy. Eternal types at the circus. The noise was terrific, the air dense with the aura of unwashed humanity. This aura was twin to the aura in a monkey-house. But I enjoyed my "bath of multitude," as Charles Baudelaire names it, and I should not have bothered the tall creature with such an inept question. She coldly regarded me:

"No, I haven't seen Hedda to-day, but I remember George Tesman always teased her with one question, 'What do you know about that, Hed?' Shoo! Sardou for mine." "Do you read George Blarney Shaw?" I persisted. "He ought to be in a cage here. He would draw some crowds. But I'm told he lives in Germany now on account of the beer." I backed away quickly as an East Side family consisting of a baker's dozen would allow. Why had I asked such a question of a perfect stranger? This

BEDOUINS

giantess, I mused before the rhinoceros with the double prongs, is Finnish. That's why she knew the name of Hedda Gabler. Why didn't I speak of Rosmersholm? Rebecca West had Finnish blood in her veins. Careful, careful— this Ibsen obsession must be surmounted, else I shall be inquiring of the giraffe if neck or nothing is the symbol of Brand. All or Nothing! of course. How stupid of me. Among the animals I regained my equilibrium. Their odors evoked memories. Yes, I recalled the old-time circus, with its compact pitched canvas tent on North Broad Street, Philadelphia; the pink lemonade, the hoarse voice of the man who entreated us to buy tickets—there were no megaphones in those days—the crisp crackling of the roasting peanuts, the ovens revolved by the man from Ravenna, the man from Ascoli, and the man from Milan. They followed the circus all the way from Point Breeze, and I swear they were to me far more human than the policemen who gently whacked us with their clubs when we crawled under the tent.

The sense of smell is first aid to memory. As I passed the cages saluting our pre-Adamic relatives, bidding the time of day to the zebu, nodding in a debonair fashion to the yak, I could not help longing for my first circus. Again I saw myself sitting in peaceful agony on a splintery plank; again I felt the slaps and pinches of my tender-hearted Aunt Sue—now in Paradise, I hope; again my heart tugged like

CHOPIN OR THE CIRCUS?

a balloon at its moorings as the clowns jumped into the ring, grimacing, chortling, and fascinating us with their ludicrous inhumanity.

Other days, other ways. I sighed as I tore myself loose from the prehensile trunk of a too friendly baby elephant and passed into the huge auditorium where Gilmore had played. Ah! the sad, bad, glad, dear, dead, tiresome, poverty-stricken, beautiful days when we were young imbeciles and held hands with a fresh "ideal" every week (sometimes two). Ah! the sentimental "jag" induced by peanut eating, and the chaste, odoriferous apes.

It is time. We seat ourselves. I look about me. Two resplendent gentlemen wearing evening clothes at high noon, after the daring manner of our Gallic cousins, toll a bell. I became excited. Why those three-and-thirty strokes? What the symbolism! Chopin, or Ibsen; again, I groaned, and turned my attention to my neighbors, one of whom I could feel, though did not see. I raised my voice, employing certain vocables hardly fit to print. The effect was magical. "Johnny, take your feet out of the gentleman's collar. That's a good boy." It was the soothing voice of a mother. Bless her clairvoyance! I sat comfortably back in my seat. Johnny howled at the interference with his pleasure. I felt sorry for him. Childhood is ever individualistic, even pragmatic. But I only had one collar with me, and it was well the matter ended thus.

BEDOUINS

Hurrah! Here they come! A goodly band. The clowns! the clowns! Some hieratic owl of wisdom has called the clown the epitome of mankind. He certainly stands for something, this "full-fledged fool," as good old Tody Hamilton used to write, and "surcharged with the Roe of Fun," which phrase beats Delaware shad. Odds fish! There was only one Hamilton. What a Rabelaisian list of names boast these merry clowns! If the years have passed over the skulls of these lively rascals, the jolly boys do not show them. The same squeaks, the identical yodling, the funny yet sinister expression of the eyes, the cruel, red-slitted mouths—not a day older than ten did I seem as they came tumbling in and began their horse-play, punctuated with yelling, yahoo gestures, ribald ejaculations, and knock-about diversions. It must all mean something, this hooting, in the economy of the universe, else "life is a suck and a sell," as Walt Whitman puts it. As in a dream-mirror I saw Solness slowly mount the fatal tower when Hilda Wangel cries to him: "My—my Masterbuilder!" She sings The Maiden's Wish, and he hears the harps of Chopin hum in the air. I rub my ears. It is not Hilda who is crying, but a pet pig in a baby carriage, wheeled by a chalk-faced varlet. How difficult it is to escape the hallucinations of the critical profession. I couldn't forget Chopin or Ibsen, even at the circus.

It was a relief, after more bellmanship from

CHOPIN OR THE CIRCUS?

the man with the shiny silk hat and spiked coat, when the elephants majestically entered. Followed the horses. Tumblers and wire-walkers, women who stood on their heads and smiled —as they do in life, something like the "inverted pyramid," as James Hinton called modern civilization—plastic poseurs, Oriental jugglers, the show was let loose at last. Human projectiles were launched through mid air to the tap of a drum. My nerves forbade me to look at them, so I read a programme advertisement of wallpaper for bathrooms. Some people like such horrible sights. I do not. They dare not precisely formulate to themselves the wish that "something" would happen, and if it does they shudder with sadistic joy. I close my eyes when the Whirl of Death or any other sensational act is staged. "Something" might happen.

The mad dancers delight our rhythmic sense as they make marvellous arabesques. The chariot races stir the blood. The crash around curves, the patters of gleaming metal excite so that you stand up, and, brushing the feet of inevitable Johnny from your neck (notwithstanding his remonstrances), you shout with woolly mouth and husky voice. Instinctively you turn down your thumbs: "Pollice verso," which Bayard Taylor translated "the perverse police." You remember the Gérôme painting?

"This beats Ibsen," I hilariously exclaimed to Johnny's mother. (She was a comely matron.) "His name is John, and when he gets home his father will beat him," she tartly replied. With the prevoyance of boyhood Johnny burst into despairing howls. I at once folded up my mind. A million things were happening in the haze of the many rings. The New Circus is polyphonic, or naught.

Enough! Filled to the eyes with the distracting spectacle, ear-drums fatigued by the blare and bang of the monster brass band, my collar quite wilted by Johnny's shoemaker, my temper in rags because of the panting, struggling army of fellow beings, I reached the avenue in safety, perspiring, thirsty, unhappy. Like Stendhal, after his first and eagerly longed-for battle with love, I exclaimed: "Is that all?" In sooth, it had been too much. The human sensorium is savagely assaulted at the twentieth century circus. I was in pessimistic enough humor to regret the single ring, the antique japes of a solitary clown, and the bewitching horsemanship of Mlle. Leonie, with her gauze skirts and perpetual rictus. As a matter of fact, we wouldn't endure for five minutes the old-fashioned circus and its tepid lemonade. Where are the mullygrubs of yesteryear? But the human heart is perverse. It always longs for the penny and the cake in company, while ineluctable destiny separates them ever. Perhaps my editor was right. Render unto Chopin the things that are Chopin's; send Ibsen back to his Land of the Midnight Whiskers. Smell the sawdust at the

CHOPIN OR THE CIRCUS?

Garden, not forgetting that the chilly, dry days are at hand when even Panem et Circenses shall be taboo; when pipe and prog and grog will be banned; when these United States shall have been renamed Puritania; when a fanatically selfish minority shall take all the joy from life. Ergo, carpe diem! I thank you.

XIV

CARUSO ON WHEELS

THAT trip was all the fault of Billy Guard, better known to the musical world as Signor Guglielmo Guardi—though no relative of the famous painter of Venetian waterscapes by the same name; it is even rumored that Guardi originally hails from the "Ould Dart," but that knotty question will be solved, no doubt, by future historians. He is none the less 110-percent American in the shade. However, to my story. I was standing in the concourse of the Pennsylvania Station when Billy interrupted my meditation on the evils of near-beer. "Are you going with us?" he hospitably inquired. I was about to board the regular three o'clock train to Philadelphia and I cheerfully accepted his invitation. And then something happened. Not far from us a circle of spectators enclosed as a focal point the natty person of Enrico Caruso and a Red Cross girl. Evidently curiosity had ascended to the blood-heat mark of the human thermometer. With difficulty was the mass kept from swamping the border of safety, and, literally, embracing the well-beloved Italian tenor. What was he doing in such a place at the uncanny hour of 2.30 P. M.?

CARUSO ON WHEELS

Singers operate their throats all night and sleep out the daylight. It was not difficult to guess that he was going to Philadelphia on the Metropolitan Opera House Special, which during the season leaves every Tuesday afternoon at 2.54, returning some time after 2 o'clock the next morning. The present intermezzo piqued my interest. I shouldered my diminutive frame through the mob, exclaiming, "Tickets, please!" and because of this official camouflage soon reached the centre of attraction. Attired in garb of fashionable hue and cut, Signor Caruso held earnest converse with a pretty Red Cross nurse, whose face beamed with joy. Something had been given which pleased her sense of the fitness of things, and later I heard that Caruso had enrolled the names of his two sons as members of the Red Cross Association; both lads were then fighting in the Italian army; Caruso is patriotic.

"Say, ain't dat guy Caroos?" was asked of me by one of the chaps at the news-stand. "Doesn't he get ten thousand dollars a night?" he further queried. "More," I replied. "Well, he don't look it," came the unexpected comment. Young America thus paid tribute to the absence of fuss and feathers in the personality of the singer. It is true Caruso does not look like the typical tenor of Italian opera, nor does he behave like one. There he was, happy as a boy out on a lark, the dingy December day not depressing him, and his spirits so high that we expected him to waltz with that gentle nurse on the finest dancing esplanade in the world. Nor did the young lady seem averse from the diversion. To the disappointment of the crowd—by this time grown to monstrous size—Caruso did not dance, contenting himself with lustily carolling a basketful of precious high notes as he descended to his drawing-room car. Manager Gatti-Casazza would have shuddered if he had been present. His supreme vocal planet prodigally wasting his golden wind in a hall bigger than the Metropolitan Opera House and no box-office in view! Besides, it was flying in the face of nature. Tenors always bundle up to the eyebrows; they do not speak, much less vocalize, and usually are as cross as the proverbial bear. Caruso, who has defied doctors and vocal hygiene since he opened his magical mouth, is a false beacon to other singers. His care-free behavior should be shunned by lesser men who attempt to bend the bow of this great singing Ulysses.

But Caruso is careful about tobacco. He does not enter the compartment where others smoke. He prefers the odor of his own choice cigarettes. I never saw him without one, either in mouth or fingers. The despair he is of any throat specialist. He sits in company with his old friend, Signor Scognomillo, otherwise the Man-Mountain. Sits and smokes. He is to sing and so he doesn't talk, only smokes, or makes caricatures. Returning is another tale. In

CARUSO ON WHEELS

hilarious mood, he orders carte-blanche supper for the chorus. He plays pranks on his fellow passengers. Even that most potent, grave, and bearded Signor, Manager Gatti, is forced to smile. Caruso is irresistible. He recalls the far-away days when he sang two operas every Sunday in the Teatro Mercadante at Naples or the good old summer-time at Salerno, when, during entr'actes, he would drop a string from his dressing-room window and draw up the fond prize—sardine and cream-cheese sandwiches. He was thin in those youthful days, and thin boys always have hollow legs that must be filled. Prosperity has not spoiled Caruso. He is human and tolerant, with a big heart, and he is devoid of professional megalomania. In common with oldsters I have railed betimes at altered musical tastes and often declared that in the days of my youth there were better singers. I still abide by this belief. There were vocal giants in those days; but there was not Enrico Caruso.

Since my dear old friend Italo Campanini there has been no one to match Caruso. Italo was a greater actor, indeed more versatile. His Lohengrin, the first I ever heard, I shall never forget. Mr. Finck is happy in his suggestion that Caruso add Lohengrin to his long list of operatic portraits. I have heard tenors from Brignoli to Gayarre, from Campanini to Tamagno, Masini and Nicolini—this second husband of Aunt Adelina Patti wasn't such a mediocrity as represented by some critics; he suffered only from contiguity to a blazing star of the first magnitude—yet no one possessed a tithe of the vocal richness of Camerado Enrico. Some have outpointed him in finesse, Bonci; Tamagno could have outroared him; Jean de Reszke had more personal charm and artistic subtlety; nevertheless, Caruso has a marvellous natural voice, paved with lyric magic. It is positively torrential in its outpouring, and with the years it grows as mellow as a French horn. Why, there are men in this vast land of ours who would rather be Caruso than the President of the United States of Europe. Can you blame them? In his golden prime, happily mated, full of verve, gayety—and healthy—well, his presence, apart from his art, consoles us for many a gray day on this ocky little orb we inhabit.

The recognition of personality has become in my "middle-years" a veritable obsession. With Henry James I could say that "I have found myself, my life long, attaching values to every noted thing in respect to a great person." Please strike out "great" from this sentence and substitute "any"; any person is interesting to me. Himself exquisitely aware of the presence of others, Henry James placed his fastidious preference amid certain castes, social and artistic. Like Walt Whitman, I prefer the company of "powerful uneducated persons," and nothing inhuman or human is foreign to me. I

CARUSO ON WHEELS

shouldn't be surprised to find more interesting "stories" among the members of the chorus than in the ranks of the "stars"; but the "stars" alone capture the curiosity of the public, and thus it is that I speak of some of them to-day instead of la bella ragazzina in Mr. Setti's forces. I was bundled on Manager Gatti's special car and promptly paid my fare to a conductor who suspiciously appraised my presence; to him I was neither fish nor flesh, nor good red chorus. I should have liked very much to walk through the chorus car, but with Otto Weil on one side and Edward Ziegler on the other I couldn't escape; furthermore, young Ziegler thus admonished me: "Sir, it's no place for an elderly inflammable person, is that car full of pretty young song-birds; Patti and Scalchi en herbe." I meekly submitted and found myself in a smoking-compartment where a card-table was promptly installed.

A friendly game of old cat bridge-whist. Now, I play Bach inventions every morning, but I can't play cards. I despise card games, agreeing with my friend J. K. Huysmans, who asserted that a monument should be erected to the memory of the inventor of cards because "he did something toward suppressing the free exchange of human imbecility." If the distinguished French pessimist and master of jewelled prose could have been with us that day he might have revised his polite judgment. Such gabbling. Such "kachesse," such feminine squabbles. No hotel piazza on the Jersey coast of an August afternoon could have held a candle to the shrewd repartee and vivacious wrangling over a few painted pasteboards. Antonio Scotti, drumming on the table the rhythm of the Rataplan, would suddenly scowl, and, with Scarpia-like intensity, demand: "Why you play that ace?" And Technical Director Siedle would groan in reply. A flash of lightning from a blue sky. Then Otto Weil banged down his cards and audibly expressed his opinion of his partner's playing. It is not fit to print. Judels never turned a hair, and he isn't bald. Even Scotti relaxed for a moment his ferocious Neapolitan air. No one can "stay mad" long with Judels. Pan Ordynski drops in, and Amato, Chalmers, or Althouse. Scotti is smokeproof. It is pleasant to record that this big operatic organization with its divers nationalities is en route a happy family. Music, after all, is the solvent, the real melting-pot of which we hear so much and see so little in every-day life.

Caruso is not the only funmaker on the wheels of this Opera Special. Rosina Galli of the dainty, tapering toes and woven paces is always rollicksome. Her imitations would make her fortune in vaudeville. Signor Gatti philosophically reposes after the fatigue of travel and Union League Club terrapin. Scotti munches chicken, resting after his Sergeant Sulpizio

From a photograph by De Strelecki

ROSINA GALLI AS THE PRINCESS IN "LE COQ D'OR"

CARUSO ON WHEELS

rôle, and still strums the Rataplan. Caruso smokes. Friend Scognomillo sleeps with one eye open. Florence Easton, wrung from her triumph as Santuzza, is there. In a compartment sits Geraldine Farrar. She sips coffee. Her mother is with her. So are chicken sandwiches. "Our Jerry" is bright-eyed and keyed up as might be expected. I mention the name "Sid" Farrar, my boyhood's idol. The ladies become sympathetic. When I stoutly declared that I had never fallen in love with a prima donna during four decades as a music reporter, my "specialty" being admiration of the mothers of singers, the air is charged with interrogation-marks. Why hasn't some authoritative pen been employed in behalf of the mother of the singer who has succeeded? What a theme! What peeps into a family inferno! I think that Mrs. Farrar could write a better book about her brilliant daughter than did Mrs. Lou Tellegen of herself.

Another time I talk with Frieda Hempel, who is one of the rapidly dwindling race of artists who know Mozart as well as Donizetti. What a Marguerite she would be! On the train she is like her contemporaries. She sits. She chats. For all I know, she may doze. Singers are very human. To fancy them as "gloomy, grand, and peculiar" is to imagine a vain thing. In private they behave like their butchers, bakers, candlestick makers. If they have one weakness peculiar to their tribe, it is never to read newspaper criticism of their performances! This is discouraging for music-critics. But the public likes sentimental flimflam, and the opera singer is pictured as a strange and fearful bird of prey; when seen at close range she is in reality a domesticated fowl. The much-advertised artistic temperament is only intermittent; even arrant bohemians are normal at least twice every twenty-four hours.

The call is sounded. Again New York! A jumble of voices is heard in the smoking-compartment. "If you hadn't played that trump!" —it is Judels speaking. "Oh!" groans Papa Siedle. Scotti is now whistling the Rataplan. The blond Ordynski, having wished the Polish curse on Otto Weil—"may you have hangnails and dandruff!"—dons his greatcoat. "Addio, Hunekero!" sings Caruso. After refusing Ned Ziegler's kind offer of "First Aid to Flatbushers," which means his private car, I find myself alone on the chilly concourse. The hour of disillusionment, three past midnight. I've been on and off wheels with Caruso for twelve times sixty minutes. I ponder Flatbush and the possibilities of getting there by dawn. The scrubwomen are at work, a new postwoman saunters along. The luncheon-room cat rubs against me, almost coos with joy. I slink away, being superstitious regarding cherry-colored cats, stepladders, and cross-eyed theatre managers. (I

CARUSO ON WHEELS

am writting plays.) Then, resigned to the inevitable, I seek my trusty Glenn Curtiss hydro-aeroplane, which is anchored in the Thirty-third Street enclosure, and fly home to Flatbush-by-the-Sea. I've had a crowded and enjoyable day.

XV
SING AND GROW VOICELESS

SING and grow voiceless! Why not? We know of a dozen methods that are guaranteed to ruin even a Rose Ponselle vocal equipment in thirty lessons by mail, better known as absent treatment. We have had over forty years' experience in the fair land of song, a scarred battle-field strewn with the shards and wrecks of beautiful voices and high hopes. In no sphere of music are there so many sharks, cormorants, swindlers, humbugs, criminals, as in the ranks of vocal teaching — so-called. The hard-earned, carefully saved money of parents is extorted from victims, who usually return home with health impaired, voices gone, even worse. It is pitiful. It is cruel. What are you going to do about it? The profession of medicine is protected. Why not music? Malpractice is swiftly punished. Why not lock up the rascals who ruin a voice and get money under false pretenses? No, chewing gum in public is of far more importance to people; now a national neurosis, it will soon be elevated to the dignity of a Fine Art. If we had our way we should drive every one of these vocal parasites who in-

SING AND GROW VOICELESS

fest the temple of music into the swamp of public odium.

Now, having worked off my chronic bad humor, let us look at the matter through the spectacles of the absurd. There is a comic side to everything, from a volcano to a prohibitionist. The fake singing-teachers are as funny as their fakery is pernicious.

I am reminded of all the pamphlets from How to be Happy Though Divorced, How to Starve and Grow Fat when I read the pompous pronouncements of certain Voice Builders. I confess that I am not an expert in vocal hygiene, but I have heard all the great men and women for the past half-century who have made this drab, dreary planet worth living on with their beautiful voices. And that is a brevet of taste. Standards. Without standards we critically perish, says, in effect, Mr. Brownell. I also confess that I don't know a resonator from a refrigerator, or the difference between a lynx and a larynx. Both growl, I believe, if you rub them the wrong way. I have not the science of W. J. Henderson or Holbrook Curtis. But I do know when a singer slathers her phrases or sings above or below pitch—and there are more who sing sharp than you think. The main thing is that I criticise by ear, not with a laryngoscope or a mirror to peep at the breath-control.

Herbert Witherspoon, not unknown to fame as an operatic artist and concert singer, summed up for me the situation in a phrase. "Opera

BEDOUINS

singers open their mouths too wide." Hence screaming and bawling which nearly splits sensitive ears. That the public likes shouting on top-tones is only evidence of the public's appalling taste. Noise, noise, noise! We worship noise in America. Another neurosis. Noise the Ultimate Vulgarity. At last the subway voice has penetrated our opera-houses; charmless, voiceless, vicious. The three dramatic unities in the modern theatre have resolved themselves into Legs, Glitter, Buncombe. On the lyric stage the chief unit is yelling. No wonder they sing and grow voiceless. Purdon Robinson, himself a concert singer of note, in the course of an instructive lecture recently remarked: "My own opinion, backed by thirty years of singing and teaching, has resulted in the belief that a mechanical method makes a mechanical singer"; and "after the voice has been placed and one has it under control, forget it when singing. Try to get at the composer's meaning, realizing that words in themselves mean little, and that notes in music are simply the symbols by which musical ideas are indicated." For the average vocalist words are not symbols but cymbals. But Mr. Robinson's words are golden.

Years ago (do sit still a moment, this is not a spun-out story of my life!) a young woman consulted me about a vocal master. She was a choir singer from the remote South, her parents poor as brewery mice—are to be—and she thought

SING AND GROW VOICELESS

she had a remarkable voice. I say "thought." Care killed a cat. Thought never slew a larynx. I played a hymn tune. She sang. I shuddered, but was relieved when she told me that her name was Elvina Crow. After all, there is something to be said for Prof. Slawkenbergius and his theory of names as set forth by the veracious Rev. Laurence Sterne. I suggested that if she decided on a career she change her name to "Sgallinacciare," which appropriately enough means to crow; also a faulty method of singing. "Signorina Sgallinacciare!" How that would ring in the credulous ears of the dear old deluded public, which, Hamlet-like, doesn't know a hawk from a hand-saw, or, if you prefer, a hernshaw. Shriek and grow rich! Nothing else matters but "mazuma" in the box-office of the Seven Deadly Arts.

It must have been a month after our interview that Miss Crow again visited me. I was at the time assistant professor of applied paleontology, and mightily interested in the psychic life of micro-organisms, so naturally singers came first on the list. Into my large and sympathetic tympani Elvina poured a tale, not of woe, but of thrilling truth. This is not the first time I have related it, yet it improves on repetition, just because of its probability. Not discouraged by my slurring, even portamento, criticism of her voice, the lone girl bravely started to find out the truth herself; the real test of character. She said that her first experience was in the studio of a maestro. She had a letter to him which he barely read. In a rich Italian brogue he bade her be seated. He wore a velvet jacket. He was bald. He smoked cigarettes. The type was perfect.

"I giva da lesson in fiva minuta," he explained, and then scowled at a tall girl who faced a mirror in a guilty manner as her eyes computed the possible value of the newcomer's gown. "Must I sit here like a fool?" the professor angrily demanded. His pupil opened her mouth. Elvina eagerly listened. But no sound escaped the lips of the other girl. She gazed into the mirror and mouthed and grimaced, and almost, though not quite, formed words. "Faster," cried the teacher at the keyboard. The student's lips moved like a praying mill; she clicked her teeth castanet fashion; and at last with a wild bang on the keyboard the voiceless aria ended. The maestro knitted his dyed eyebrows. "Vara fair, not presto assai. You sing without expression. You are too cold — what shall I call it?" A husky voice asked: "Shall I try it over again?" "Dio mio! girl, how dare you speak after singing such a difficult aria from Rossini's Cinderella? Your vocal pores are open, you perspire with your lungs — pouf! You die of the inflammatus by, by" — he impatiently pulled at his large nose. "The Inflammatus by Rossini, you mean!" interposed Elvina. "How? No, no, ah! by pneumonia, that's it." And he bustled from the instrument. Throwing an old bearskin

SING AND GROW VOICELESS

rug over his speechless singer, he led her to a chair, admonishing her: "Now perspire!" She coughed in a terrifying way while the maestro imperturbably explained his method to Elvina. He did not permit his pupils to open their mouths for a year, during which time he put them through a severe throat and lung drill. All songs were given in vocal miming, with due facial expression, and the ventriloquist was adduced as the highest type of masterly vocal control, for a ventriloquist can sing in his stomach without moving a muscle of his face. Think of Fred Stone and his Very Good Eddie. The Signor became eloquent. Had the young Miss Elvina — Corpo di Baccho! what a pretty name! — had she a little money for tuition? One thousand dollars. Dirt cheap. A second Patti she would become for the money. Sign a contract with him for ten years. Then the movies for a year so that her stage nervousness would wear off, then vaudeville, et puis donc — grand opera. A ravishing prospect. He rolled his eyes ecstatically as he took Elvina's ten-dollar bill. She escaped. To her taste the method seemed a trifle too swift.

In another part of the town she found the atelier of Mme. Boche. She was about to enter the anteroom unannounced when she heard low moaning sounds, which presently increased in volume and intensity, then suddenly died away in a sickening style. It seemed as if some animal were undergoing vivisection, and Elvina, her sympathies aroused, pushed open the door without knocking. It was a strange sight that met her indignant gaze, a sight that set her wondering, and soon smiling. On a huge mattress, which occupied half the room, were a dozen girls in seaside bathing costume. They lay on their backs, and upon their diaphragms rested twenty-pound weights, and from their closed lips issued the moans made by their respiration. The Madame, a high-nosed old dame, stood by, rattan cane in hand, and in militarist accents gave her commands: "One, two, three—inhale! Hold breath! Shoulders—up! Relax! Down!" And the class went patiently through this ventral drill until completely fagged. After the order to arise a babel of chatter ensued as Elvina told the Madame of her aspirations and the amount of cash she possessed.

"Na! I have the only system for the breathing. My pupils know how to breathe, how to breathe, and, again—how to breathe. There is one necessary thing in singing, the breath. If my pupils can't stand my system I send them forth."

Elvina positively feared this martinet. Her pupils' figures were lanky. She mildly inquired when they sang. "What, sing? Niemals, never, jammai, jamais de la leben! You heard them breathing? Did they breathe or no?" Then turning to her class she resumed: "Young ladies, attention! Fall down! Relax!" Elvina slipped

SING AND GROW VOICELESS

away, muttering as she went: "Calisthenics, not art." It had cost her another ten dollars.

After a hurried Automat luncheon she proceeded to a crosstown street, the address of which she had read in the newspapers. The window displayed this sign, "Professor Erasmus Brick, Voice Builder." He was a burly gentleman, the Prof. His linen was not irreproachable, his forehead looked like a mansard roof, and his eyes were shrewd. She named her errand, confided her doubts, hinted at the poverty of her purse. He laughed, and his voice restored her courage, if not her confidence. "My dear Miss, cast your eye round this room and see if I have a piano, a looking-glass, a pulsometer, or any other foreign fiddle-faddle of those Signors or Fraus. I build the voice up into the perfect thing the good Lord intended it to be, and without any extry fixin's or bricks and mortar. The job is simple if you know how. All this gabble about vocal registers and nasal emission makes me tired. I build up a voice on the word 'Moo'; jest keep 'em right at that word till the old cow—so to speak—dies of the tune. While you sing I work this pocket-fan. I use it to fan away the breath as you sing 'Moo.' By this means the lungs are unobstructed and the voice grows of its free accord. My theory is that the breath kills the voice— Moo!" Elvina passed out, and in the hall a phonograph hoarsely sang: "Do, re, mi, fa, sol.

Five dollars. Please put the cash on the mantelpiece." "That's a dollar a note," she calculated. She paid, and her bank-roll became ominously slender.

She found Mlle. Pinson in her apartment, small, stuffy, crowded with rickety furniture, books, china, music, even a parrot. The lady was drinking chocolate. "V'là, Mamselle! I've purchased a frugal meal, is it not? I diet myself as carefully as in the days when I was leading soprano at the Grand Opera. Hélas! those miserable days when I was so happy. Oh, Paris! Now sing 'la,' Mamselle. No, no, louder, please. C'est bon. You must know that when you sing correctly the vibrations travel to the knee-caps. I test them and know exactly if the tone is formed naturally or not. My vibratory system is the only true one. Yes, twenty dollars will be enough for this time. You have a sweet voice, my dear, and I'll make a great singer of you in five years." Elvina faintly asked: "When do I begin on songs?" "What! Songs? Ah! those Americans, they are always in a hurry, what you call get rich in a week! My child, you can't hurry art. Bonsoir, Mamselle! Tomorrow at nine, precisely, and I'll test your knee-caps. Take one of my pamphlets. Vibration, vibration, vibration!" The parrot opened its beak: "Vibration, vibration, vibration. I'm in for life, chérie. Take me out of jail, chérie." Elvina sat in a Madison Avenue tram and read the booklet of Mlle. Mimi Pinson, entitled Hy-

SING AND GROW VOICELESS

giene for Voiceless Singers. Numerous rules and "Don'ts," ending with, "Don't marry. Husbands of opera-singers always collect their wives' salaries. Vibrate when you breathe. You may achieve fame and happiness. Think blue! It is the color of hope. Vogue la galère!"

"This is becoming monotonous," said Elvina aloud, and gritting her teeth she packed her duds and returned to her home town with only one dollar and twenty-five cents in her pocket. However, family affection, above all family flapjacks, restored her jarred nerves to their normal pitch. From time to time she sends me programmes of concerts in which she is described: "Our native song-bird, Elvina, Prima Donna Dissoluta." As Esther Beautiful Queen (newly reorchestrated by Stravinsky) she made a "real hit." She may have exaggerated a little in her confidences, but I can personally vouch for the heavy weights on pupils' chests to promote breathlessness. There was advocated such a vocal system two or three decades ago in New York. Sing and grow voiceless! Basta!

XVI
ANATOLE FRANCE: THE LAST PHASE

ANATOLE FRANCE is seventy-six years old, but his mind is still vigorous, if that word be not too brisk when applied to such a subtle, supple, undulating intelligence as his. He now writes prose glowing with patriotism. Like the late Remy de Gourmont he shed his cynic's skin when war invaded his beloved land. And it was not the first time that he, a writer of humanitarian impulses, opened the door of his ivory tower and descended into the stormy arena; witness the Dreyfus case. However, it would be idle to deny that his best work is well behind him. Prefaces to letters to distinguished men and women he occasionally publishes, such as Sur la Voie Glorieuse, or Ce que disent nos morts; but the Anatole France of La Révolte des Anges seems to have vanished forever. In the vast whirlwind of European events his scepticism, irony, and pessimism have given way to pity and tenderness for human suffering. The son of the bookseller Thibaut may figure, some day, in a modern hagiography of those laysaints who fought for a new spiritual freedom.

The subject-matter composing Sur la Voie

ANATOLE FRANCE

Glorieuse is altogether patriotic and contains much that is striking. The cloven hoof of the original faun that lurks somewhere in this Frenchman's temperament is shown in a passage wherein he groups the Christmas festival with other antique festivals and symbols of Adonis and Mithra. A pagan to the end. Possibly the best pages are devoted to a free translation from Herodotus, a dialogue between the potentate Xerxes and a Spartan slave. The moral rings clear. Of quite different material is fashioned The Revolt of the Angels. We cannot conscientiously recommend the fiction to elderly persons of either sex, though, no doubt, it is favorite reading of the "advanced" college girl. What would be vulgarity in another writer is turned to favor and prettiness by the wand of the Gallic enchanter. Violence, rapine, hissing irony, and Rabelaisian episodes make a feast for lovers of Anatolian literature. Those who have retained any old-fashioned prejudices concerning propriety — morality is out of the running — may expect to be shocked. Has he not said: "Man, seek not to know thyself! Man is not a reasoning animal."

In this fable the deity that created us is in the new cosmology only a tribal god, who, since he deposed Lucifer in pitched battle, rules tyrannically. He keeps close watch on our mud-pie of a planet because he suspects that numerous angels disguised as men and women are fomenting a second angelic rebellion. With them are the socialists and anarchists, and this gives M. France an opportunity to score monarchical forms of government. The clerical order is lashed. He spares no one. He repeats his familiar axiom: "Les guerres sont toujours les affaires." There are pages in which sensuality and sheer burlesque are mingled in a disquieting compound. The book is one of the most daring. In its essence it is a supreme revolt against all social systems that uphold slavery: industrial, militaristic, religious, political. The debasing Asiatic systems that still make captive the conscience of mankind are mercilessly attacked, and while the castigating hand is incased in velvet the shining steel is none the less deadly.

Constable, the English landscapist, said that a good thing can't be done twice. Anatole France has demonstrated the contrary in his latest, let us hope not his last book, Le Petit Pierre, another series of exquisite notations of childhood. His delightful Livre de Mon Ami gave us glimpses of his early days. Fascinating are the chapters devoted to Pierre and Suzanne in this memoir. The tenderness of M. France, and his power of summoning up the wonder and awe of our youth, may be seen in Abeille; the development of the lad is followed in Pierre Nozière. A portrait of the young Anatole reveals his excessive sensibility. His head was large, the brow too broad for the feminine chin, though the long nose and firm mouth contradict possible weakness in the lower part of the face. It was in the eyes that the future of the child might have been read—they were lustrous, in shape beautiful, with a fulness that argued eloquence and imagination. Such eyes were possessed by the boy Charles Dickens. France has told us that he was a strange child, whose chief ambition was to be a saint, a second St. Simon Stylites, and after that thrilling experience to write a history of France in fifty volumes! In Le Petit Pierre his memory for the important little events of a child's existence is unusual; evidently nothing has been invented, all happened. Through the haze of the immemorial years there now and then sharply shines some significant incident, some old wives' tales, a portrait of an elderly contemporary — like the Balzacian Uncle Hyacinthe or the incomparable evocation of the beloved servant Mélanie—a dog, like Caire, the truant parrot, the boy chimney-sweep, and the sweet smile of Pierre's mother, who seems to be every one's mother so admirably generalized is the type — what a magician is this writer! Told with naïveté and verve, we feel in every page of Le Petit Pierre the charm of personality.

In clarity Anatole France is the equal of Renan and John Henry Newman, and, while at one time clarity was a conventional quality of French prose, it is rarer to-day. Symbolism has supervened, if not to darken counsel, certainly to trouble verbal values. Never syncopated, moving at a moderate tempo, in transitions smooth, replete with sensitive rejections, crystalline in diction, a lover and a master of large, luminous words, the very marrow of the man, Anatole France is in his style. And what a model he should be for those wilful young writers who boast that lumpy, graceless paragraphs are better suited to their subjects than swift, clear, concise prose. It was not so long ago that one scribe positively glorified in his own dull style; he asserted that it was a truthful reflection of his drab themes. There is, indeed, such a thing as an apposite garbing, a verbal orchestration. The pellucid sentences of Mr. Howells, so free from the overblown, are happily wedded to his admirable character etching. Flaubert, master of ornate, or "numerous" prose, as well as cool, rhythmic prose, wrote Salammbô in a purple, splendid key, and Madame Bovary in the greyer tonalities of the province; yet nothing could be further removed from the style of either novel than Sentimental Education, which is urban and suffused with sober daylight. It was a favorite contention of de Gourmont that at his sovereign best Flaubert is to be found in Bouvard et Pécuchet, the style of which is sinewy, pregnant, powerful. The principal mistake of beginners is to believe that ornament is good style. In Anatole France matter and manner are perfectly welded.

Few writers swim so easily as he under their heavy burdens of erudition. His knowledge is precise, his range wide. He is a humanist. He

ANATOLE FRANCE

knows many literatures. He loves learning for the sake of learning. He loves words, treasures them, fondles them, burnishes anew their meanings tarnished by custom. He seldom tarries in the half-way house of epigram. Over all, his interest in humanity sheds a tranquil glow. Without a marked feeling for the dramatic, nevertheless, he surprises mankind engaged in its minute daily acts; those he renders as candidly as snow in the sunshine; just as the old Dutch painters stir our "emotion of recognition" with a simple shaft of light passing through a half-open door, or upon an old wrinkled woman polishing her spectacles. He sees and notes many gestures, inutile or tragic, and notes them with the enthralling simplicity of a complicated artistic nature. He deals with ideas so vitally that they seem human. Yet his personages are never abstractions, nor do they serve as pallid allegories. They are all alive from Sylvestre Bonnard to the group that meets to chat in the Foro Romano (Sur la Pierre Blanche); from his Penguins to his Angels. A dog, a cat, he depicts with the same love; his dog Riquet bids fair to endure in literature. France is an interpreter of life, not precisely after the manner of the novelist, but life as viewed through the temperament of a poet of extreme delicacy and one doubled by a tolerant philosopher.

This ultramodern thinker, who has outgrown the despotism of positivist dogma, has the soul of a chameleon. He loves, he understands,

BEDOUINS

Christianity with a fervor and a knowledge that surprise, until we measure the depth of his affection for antique cultures. Further to confuse us, he exhibits sympathy with the Hebraic lore. He has rifled the Talmud for half-forgotten tales. He delights in juxtaposing the Greek sophist and the strenuous Paul. He contrasts Mary Magdalen repentant with a pampered Roman matron. He is familiar with the proceeds of science, particularly astronomy. With the scholastic speculations of the Renaissance, with the simple affirmations of mediæval piety, he is as conversant as with the destructive pyrrhonism of a boulevard philosopher. So commingled are his contradictory cultures, so numerous his angles, so avid of impressions is he, that we end in wholly admiring the exercise of a beneficent magic that can blend into a happy synthesis moral dissonances and harmonize such a bewildering moral preciosity. But there are moments when we regard the operation as intellectual legerdemain. We suspect dupery. However, it is his humor that is the most potent of his solvents. This humor often transforms a doubtful battle into radiant victory. We see him, the protagonist of his own psychical comedy, dancing on a tight rope in the airiest fashion, deliciously capering in the metaphysical void, and, like a prestidigitator, bidding us doubt the very existence of his rope.

Proofs from life gay pagan Anatole does not demand. He has the hesitations of profound erudition. Possessing the gift of paradox, he rejoices in his philosophic indifferentism. Notwithstanding his famous phrase, "the mania of certitude," Renan was ever pursued by the idea of an Absolute. He cried for proof. To Bertholet he wrote: "I am eager for mathematics." To him numbers promised rigid reality. Not so, however, to M. France, who could have asked with Ibsen whether two added to two do not make five on the planet Jupiter! To Montaigne's "What know I?" he opposes the injunction of Rabelais: "Do what thou wilt!" Of Plato he might have asked, "What is Truth?" and if Plato in turn would have posed the same question, Anatole could reply by handing him a copy of Jardin d'Epicure, that perfect breviary of Anatolian scepticism. In Socrates perhaps he would discover a congenial companion; yet he might mischievously allude to Montaigne "concerning cats," or quote Aristotle as to the form of hats. And then we spy him adorning the Wheel of Ixion with garlands. A wilful child of belles-lettres and philosophy, M. France always may be expected to utter the starting, lucent phrase.

He believes in the belief of God. By the gods of all times and climes he swears. His the cosmic soul. A man who infuses into his tales something of the Mimes of Herondas, La Bruyère's Characters, and the Lucian Dialogues, with faint flavors of Racine and La Fontaine superadded, may be pardoned his polychromatic faiths. This chromatism in creeds, a trust in all or none, is rather diverting. But the classic world of thought shows several exemplars for M. France, from the followers of Aristippus to the Sophists. Nevertheless, there is a specific note of individuality, a roulade altogether Anatolian in the Parisian. No one but this accomplished sceptic could have devised The Opinions of Jerome Coignard, and his scheme for a Bureau of Vanity (Villiers de l'Isle Adam invented a machine for manufacturing glory). "Man is an animal with a musket," declares Anatole. Here is a morsel for hypocrites: "Even virtue may be unduly praised. Since it is overcoming which constitutes merit, we must recognize that it is concupiscence which makes saints." This sounds like William Blake done into choice French; Blake who has said that "the fool cannot enter the kingdom of heaven be he ever so pious"; that Blake who believed that the road to wisdom lies through the valley of excess.

Henry James has declared that the province of art is all life, all feeling, all observation, all vision. According to this rubric, M. France is a many-sided artist. Philosopher as well, he plays with the appearances of life, lifting betimes the edge of the curtain to curdle the blood of his spectators with the sight of Buddha's shadow in some grim cavern beyond. He shows his Gallic tact in decorating the empty spaces of theory and the blank spots of reality. A follower of Kant, in his denial of the objective, we cannot imagine him approving of that sage's admiration of the starry heavens and the moral law. Both are relative, would be the report of the Frenchman. Yet he yearns for faith. He humbles himself beneath the humblest. He excels in exposing the splendor of the simple soul, though faith has not anointed his intellect with its chrism. He admires the golden filigree of the ciborium; its spiritual essence escapes him. At the portals of Paradise he lingers, or stoops to pick a rare and richly colored feather. He eloquently vaunts its fabulous beauty. But he hears not the whirring of the wings whence it has fallen. Pagan in his irony, his pity wholly Christian, Anatole France betrays a nuance of Petronius and a touch of St. Francis. Because of this spiritual dislocation — or dare I say bilocation? — he is in art, letters, and life a consummate flowering of the dilettante.

XVII

A MASQUE OF MUSIC

HERE is an evocation of a projected Masque of Music. Not a Miltonic hymn in praise of the melting art, nor yet an Alexander's Feast celebrating its power, after the manner of John Dryden, but a grandiose vision which would embrace the legend of sound from its unorganized beginnings to the to-morrow of the ultimate Kalmuck. It is written with such men as Reinhardt, David Belasco, Gordon Craig, Stanislavsky, Michel Fokine, and Richard Ordynski in view. They, or artists of their calibre, might make the idea viable in the theatre. What music would best envelope my Masque is a question answered by the composers whose names are figuratively deployed. Or what gifted American composers might "set" the Masque in a symphonic poem! Where this kaleidoscope would be produced and how many evenings it might need for complete interpretation are puzzles I do not seek now to solve; suffice to add, that I have for the sake of dramatic unity placed myself at the centre and circumference of this prose recital, as sensations are veritable hallucinations for me. In a performance the spectators would occupy the same relative position.

A MASQUE OF MUSIC

... The curtains of Time and Space drew apart. I stood on the cliff of the World, saw and heard the travailing and groaning of light and sound in the epochal and reverberating void. A pedal-bass, a diapasonic tone that came from the bowels of the firmament, struck fear to my heart; this tone was of such magnitude as might be overheard by the gods. No mortal ear could have held it without cracking. This gigantic flood, this cataclysmic roar, filled every pore of my body. It blew me about as a blade of grass is blown in a boreal blast, yet I sensed the pitch. Inchoate nature, the unrestrained cry of the rocks and their buried secrets — crushed aspirations, and the hidden sorrows of mineral, plants, and animals became vocal. It was the voice of the monstrous abortions of nature, the groan of incomplete or transitional types, born for a moment and shattered forever. All God's mud made moan for recognition.

It was night. The strong fair sky of the South was sown with dartings of silver and starry dust. I walked under the great windbowl with its few balancing clouds and listened to the whirrings of the infinite. I knew that I was close to the core of existence, and though sound was less vibratile than light, sound touched earth, embraced it, and was content with its eld and homely face. Light, a mischievous Loge; Sound, the All-Mother Erda. I walked on. My way seemed clearer. . . .

Reaching a plain, fabulous and mighty, I

came upon a Sphinx, half-buried in sand and looming in the starlight. As I watched her face I felt that the tone had ceased to surround me. The dawn filtered through the dark and there were stirrings abroad in the air. From afar sounded a fluttering of thin tones. As the sun shone rosy on the vast stone, like a clear-colored wind came back the tone from the sea. And in the music-filled air I fell on my knees and worshipped the Sphinx, for music is a window through which we gaze upon eternity. Then followed a strange musical rout of the nations; I saw defile before me Silence, "eldest of all things"; Brahma's consort, Saraswati, fingered her Vina, and Siva and his hideous mate, Devi, sometimes called Durga; and the brazen heavens were like a typhoon that showered appalling evils upon mankind. All the gods of Egypt and Assyria, dog-faced, moon-breasted, and menacing, passed playing upon dreams, making choric music, black and fuliginous. The sacred Ibis stalked in the silvery footsteps of the Houris; the Graces held hands. Phœbus Apollo appeared. His face was as a shining shield. He improvised upon a many-stringed lyre of tortoise-shell, and his music was shimmering and symphonious. Hermes and his Syrinx wooed the shy Euterpe; the maidens went in woven paces, a medley of masques flamed by, and the great god Pan breathed into his pipes.

I saw Bacchus pursued by ravening Mænads, saw Lamia and her ophidian flute, as Orpheus

A MASQUE OF MUSIC

sorrowfully sped, searching his Eurydice. Neptune blew his wreathéd horn. The Tritons gambolled in the waves. Cybele changed her cymbals. And with his music Amphion summoned rocks to Thebes. Jepthah danced to her death before the Ark of the Covenant, praising the Lord God of Israel. Unabashed behind her leered the rhythmic Herodias, while were heard the praiseful songs of Deborah and Barak as St. Cæcilia smote the keyboard. With her timbrel Miriam sang hymns of triumph. Before the Persian Satrap on his purple litter Abyssinian girls, their little breasts carolling to the sky, alluringly swayed; the air was crowded by the crisp tinklings of tiny bells at wrist and ankles as the Kabaros drummed; and hard by in the brake brown nymphs moved in languorous rhythms, droning hoarse sacrificial chants. The colossus Memnon hymned, priests of Baal screamed as they lacerated themselves with knives, Druid priestesses crooned sybillic incantations. And over this pageant of Woman and Music the proud sun of old Egypt scattered splendid burning rays.

From distant strands and hillsides came the noise of unholy instruments with names, sweet-sounding, and clashing. Nofres from the Nile, Ravanastrons of Ceylon, Javanese gongs, Chinese Pavilions, Tambourahs, Sackbuts, Shawms, Psalteries, Dulcimers, Salpinxes, Keras, Timbrels, Sistra, Crotala, double flutes, twenty-two stringed harps, Kerrenas, the Indian flute called Yo, and the quaint Yamato-Koto. Followed fast the Biwa, the Gekkin, and its cousin the Genkwan; the Ku, named after a horrid god; the Shunga and its cluttering strings, the Samasien, the Kokyu, the Vamato Fuye — which breathed moon-eyed melodies — the Hichi-Riki, and the Shaku-Hachi. The Sho was mouthed by slant-haired yellow boys, while the sharp roll of drums covered with goatskins never ceased. From this bedlam there occasionally emerged a splinter of tune like a plank thrown up by the sea. No melody could I discern, though I grasped its beginnings. Double flutes gave me the modes: Dorian, Phrygian, Æolian, Lydian, Ionian; after Sappho and her Mixo-Lydian mode I longed for a modern accord.

The choir went whirling on with Citharas, Rebecs, Citoles, Domras, Goules, Serpents, Crwths, Pentachords, Rebabs, Pantalons, Conches, Flageolets made of Pelican bones, Tams-tams, Carillons, Xylophones, Crescents of beating bells, Mandoras, Whistling Vases of clay, Zampognas, Zithers, Bugles, Octochords, Naccaras or Turkish Castanets, and Quinternas. I heard blare the two hundred thousand curved trumpets which Solomon had made for his Temple, and the forty thousand which accompanied the Psalms of David. Jubal played his Magrephá. Pythagoras came with his Monochord. To the music of the Spheres Plato listened. The priests of Joshua blew seven times upon Shofars, or rams-horns. Then fell the walls of Jericho. To

A MASQUE OF MUSIC

this came a challenging blast from the terrible horn of Roland of Roncesvalles. The air had the resonance of hell as the Guatemalan Indians worshipped their Black Christ upon the Plaza; and naked Ishtar, Daughter of Sin, stood shivering before the Seventh Gate. A great silence ensued. I saw a green star drop over Judea and thought music itself were slain. The pilgrims with their Jew's-harps dispersed into sorrowful groups. Blackness usurped the sonorous sun. There was no music in all the universe, and this tonal eclipse lasted long. From remote coasts came faint cries: The Great God Pan is dead! They have slain Our Lord and we know not where to find Him. . . .

I heard as if in a magic mirror the submerged music of Dufay, Okeghem, Josquin Deprès, Orlando di Lasso, Goudimel, and Luther; the cathedral tones of Palestrina, the frozen sweetness of Arezzo, Frescobaldi, Monteverde, Carissimi, Tartini, Corelli, Scarlatti, Jomelli, Pergolesi, Lulli, Rameau, Couperin, Buxtehude, Sweelinck, Byrd, Gibbons, Purcell, and the Bach; with their Lutes, Monochords, Virginals, Harpsichords, Clavicytherums, Clavichords, Cembalos, Spinets, Theorbos, Organs, and Pianofortes, and accompanying them an army, vast, formidable, of the immemorial virtuosi, singers, castrati, the night-moths and midgets of music. Like wraiths they waved desperate ineffectual hands and made sad mimickings of their dead and dusty triumphs. . . . Again I heard the Chromatic Fantasia of Bach, ever new, yet old. In its weaving sonant patterns were the detonations of the primeval world I had just left; also something disquieting and feminine. But the Man predominates in Bach, subtle, nervous, magnetic as he is in this Fantasia.

A mincing, courtly old woman bows low. It is Joseph Haydn, and there is sprightly malice in his music. The glorious periwigged giant of London conducts a chorus of a million. The hailstones of Handel pelt the pate of the Sphinx. "A man!" I cried, as the very heavens stormed out their cadenced hallelujahs. A divine youth approaches. His mien is excellent, and his voice of rare sweetness. His band discourses ravishing music. The primeval tone is there, but feminized, graceful; troupes of painted stage players in fallals and furbelows present pictures of rakes, rustic maidens, and fantastics. An orchestra minces as Mozart disappears. Behold, the great one approaches, and beneath his Jovian tread the earth trembles! Beethoven, the sublime peasant, the conqueror, the god! All that has gone before, all that is to be, is globed in his symphonies, was divined by this seer. A man, the first since Handel! And the eagles triumphantly jostle the scarred face of the Sphinx. Von Weber prances by on his gayly caparisoned arpeggios, Meyerbeer and Verdi follow; all three footlight folk. Schubert, a pan-pipe through which the wind discourses exquisite melodies; Gluck, whose lyre is stringed Greek

A MASQUE OF MUSIC

fashion, but bedecked with Parisian gauds and ribbons; Mendelssohn, a charming, girlish echo of Bach; Chopin and Schumann, romantic wrestlers with their muted dreams, strugglers against ineffable madness and sorely stricken at the end; Berlioz, a primitive Roc, half-bird, half-human, also a Minotaur who dragged to his Crete all the music of the Masters; and the Turk of the keyboard, Franz Liszt, with Cymbalom, Czardas, and crazy Kalamaïkas pass. But suddenly I noted a shriller tonal accent, the accent of a sun that has lost its sex, a sun that is stricken with moon-sickness. A hybrid appears, followed by a cohort of players. A huge orchestra plays straightway; the Sphinx wears a sinister smile. . . .

Then I saw the tone-color of each instrument. Some malign enchanter had diverted from their natural uses every member of the tonal army. I saw the strings in rainbow hues, red trumpets, blue flutes, green oboes, purple clarinets, horns glorious golden yellow, scarlet trombones, darkbrown bassoons, carmilion ophecleides, as the drums punctured space with ebon crepitations. That the triangle always had been silver I never questioned, but this new chromatic blaze, these novel tintings of tone — what did they portend? Was it a symbol of the further degradation and effeminization of music? Was art become as the sigh of a woman? A vain, selfish goddess was about to be placed on high and worshipped; soon the rustling of silk would betray her sex. Released from the wise bonds imposed upon her by Mother Church, music is now a parasite of the emotions, a modern Circe whose "feet take hold on hell," whose wand enchants men into listening swine. Gigantic as antediluvian ferns, as evil-smelling and as dangerous, music in the hands of this magician is dowered with ambiguous attitudes, with anonymous gestures, is color become sound, sensuality masking as chaste beauty. This Klingsor evirates, effeminates, disintegrates. He is the spirit who denies all things natural, and his revengeful theatric music goes about in the guise of a woman. She hastens its end, its spiritual suicide is at hand. I lifted my eyes. Surely I recognized that short, dominating figure conducting the orchestra. Was it the tragic comedian, Richard Wagner? Were those his mocking, ardent eyes fading in the morbid mist?

A fat, cowled monk stealthily marches after him. He shades his eyes from the fierce rays of the Wagnerian sun; to him more grateful are moon-rays and the reflected light of lonely forest pools. He is the Arch-Hypocrite of Tone, and he speaks in divers tongues. Brahms it is and he wears the mask of a musical masquerader. Then swirled by a band of gypsies, with guitars, castanets, and led by Bizet. Spain seemed familiar land, Spain with the odors of the boudoir. Gounod and Faust go simpering on tiptoe; a disorderly mass of Cossacks stampeded them, Tchaikovsky at their head. They yelled

A MASQUE OF MUSIC

as they banged upon resounding Svirelis, Balalaikas, and Kobzas, dancing the Ziganka all the while. And as a still more horrible uproar was heard I became suddenly conscious of a change on the face of the Sphinx; streaked with grey it seemed to be crumbling. As the clatter increased I diverted my regard from the massive stone and beheld an orgiastic mob of men and women howling and playing upon instruments of fulgurating colors and vile shapes. Their skins were white, their hair yellow, their eyes of victorious blue.

"Nietzsche's Blond Barbarians, the Apes of Wagner!" I exclaimed, and I felt the ground giving away. The naked music, pulsatile and opium-charged, turned hysterical as Zarathustra-Strauss waved on his myrmidons with frenzied philosophical motions. Music was become vertiginous, a mad vortex wherein whirled mad atoms madly embracing. Dancing, the dissonant corybantes of the Dionysiac evangel scarce touched earth, thus outvying the bacchantes. The roar of enemy cannon pursued them as the last Superman yielded his ghost to the Time-Spirit. . . .

Then there gravely marched a group of men of cold cerebral expression. They carried steel hammers with which they beat upon their anvils the whole-tone scale. Near by hovered Arnold Schoenberg with Claude Debussy, but they put their fingers into their pained ears as the Neo-Scythians, Scriabine Stravinsky, Ornstein and

BEDOUINS

Prokofieff hammered with excruciating dynamics hell itself into icy enharmonic splinters. With thunderous peals of ironic laughter the Sphinx sank into the sand, yawning as it vanished and mumbling: "No longer are there dissonances. Nothing is true. All is permitted!" By a mighty effort to escape the nipping arctic air and the harsh grindings of impending icebergs, I fled.

And that is my Masque of Music.

PART II
IDOLS AND AMBERGRIS

"Idols and ambergris and rare inlays. . . ."
—*Ezra Pound.*

I
THE SUPREME SIN

"Et Diabolus incarnatus est. Et homo factus est."
—*From the Litany of the Damnèd Saints.*

"Shall no new sin be born for men's trouble?"
—*Swinburne.*

"Let us deny Satan!"
—*Sar Péladan.*

I

IDLY tapping the metal-topped table of the café with his stick, Oswald Invern waited for the Hollin boys. They had promised, the night before, to be punctual. It was past eleven and the pair had not turned up; he was bored, irritated. If they couldn't remember their engagement, well and good; but why ——!

"Oswald, have we kept you waiting?" intoned two pleasant tenor voices. There they were at last! Oswald made room for them on the divan and at once the twin brothers began smoking. Harry fetched a pipe from the bulging pocket of his coat and Willy lighted a cigarette. It was their pet affectation to pretend that they disliked any suggestion of twinship. Willy wore high heels and fashionably cut clothes so as to appear taller than his brother, while Harry sported Bohemian velvet and a broad-brimmed hat. But both agreed as to art and brotherly love. People endured them for these salient traits, though Oswald declared that it only made them the more stupid.

"No headache this morning, Oswald?"

"No heartache this morning, Oswald?"

The young man envied them as they pulled their fan-shaped beards and sipped their vermouth-citron. They were in key with the cosmos and he was not.

"Neither one nor the other," he absently replied.

"But is not Miss Tilney a charmer? I saw you looking at her the entire evening. Come now, say?" Harry Hollin spoke with enthusiasm. Invern slowly shook his head and he continued to gaze down the Boulevard de Vaugirard. The café stood at the meeting of this boulevard and the Place du Maine, across from the Gare Mont-Parnasse. The Avenue du Maine intersected the Place and, while beyond lay the choicer precincts of the Quarter, there was no spot on the "left bank" that was gayer in silent weather or duller when the rain fell. This particular morning the sky reported a delicate pigeon-blue, a nuance that occasionally may be seen in Paris after a storm; it had withdrawn above the housetops and was immeasurably far away; a melochromatic horizon was tinged with flushes of pink and ochre.

THE SUPREME SIN

The twins followed Oswald's eyes and boiled over ecstatically:

"What tones!" cried Harry.

"I could model them in precious gems!" exclaimed his brother.

"There you go, with your atelier slang," muttered their companion. "I've been in Paris ten years longer than you and you beat me as a Frenchman."

"Ça ne biche pas?" Harry continued. "It's lovely."

"Oui, c'est kif — kif!" chimed his brother. Invern watched them, the echo of a smile sounding across his compressed lips. He was not more than twenty-eight; a slender figure proclaimed his youth. The head was well set on his shoulders. It was the expression of his frowning forehead and large, dark, heavy eyes that made the man look much older. Not dissipation, rather discontent, marred features of a Byzantine type. Yes, he had been thirteen years in Paris and these foolish good-hearted fellows only three; but they knew the argot of the Beaux-Arts better than he, and they openly boasted their anti-Americanism. He asked them:

"Frankly, what are you going to do with yourselves in America — when you get there?" They answered in happy unison: "Make money."

He shook his head.

"Make money by selling tombstones — that's

you, Willy! — and painting society dames in impossible attitudes, tints, and expressions — that's you, Harry."

"Never mind us, Invern. *You* may never go, but if you do — a comic opera with a howling success is our wish."

"I'll never return — now," said Invern. "The cursed microbe of artistic Paris is in my system. And, what's more, I'll never do anything. When a Yankee comes over here to paint he tries to paint like a Frenchman. Look at the three Salons with their half-baked imitations. Let me finish" — the brothers had lifted angry shoulders — "and if a Yankee studies music here he composes French music ever afterward — French music which is a sad mixture of German and Italian; eclectic style, the wise ones call it."

"And if he goes to Germany?" demanded Harry.

"Then he composes German music." Suddenly Willy stood up.

"I have solved the mystery. This pessimism, Oswald, is the result of — of — why, you're in love, man! I know her name. It's Miss Tilney — June Tilney. The secret is out."

"Is her name June?" asked Oswald irrelevantly.

"It's June and she's rich as the sound of her name." The Hollin boys were irrepressible this gay morning.

"So! But why June?"

THE SUPREME SIN

"You're interested. Listen," interpolated Harry. "She's a Yankee girl with a Russian mother — or had one — and she was educated in London, Russia, Italy, Germany, Paris ——"

"Go on! Why not New York?"

"She never saw New York, but she speaks United States."

"And," added Willy, "the Count hates it like the dickens."

"What a pair of rattles you are! Who's the Count?"

"Why, Count Van Zorn, her guardian, of course. Haven't you met old Van Zorn yet? He's *very* musical, goes to all the swell musical Salons of Paris, to the Princesse de Brancovan, to the Comtesse de Blanzay, to Duchesse de Bellune, to the Princesse de Bibesco — " Oswald held up his hands in consternation.

"Stop! I don't care a sou where he goes. Who is he?"

"He's very rich and looks after June Tilney's affairs. And — they say — wants to marry her — only thirty years' difference — she won't have it, though she likes the old codger and is seen everywhere with him — and they say the Rasta — he's from Roumania or South America — goes in for magic and puts spells upon the girl."

"Drop the mufle," interrupted Oswald. "The main thing now is breakfast. And, incidentally, why don't you marry the girl yourself, Willy?"

"C'est à Bibi!" exclaimed Harry, pointing

to himself. "Willy has signed over all rights and interests to his loving brother. And we have the cabot on the run — he will be here in five minutes"; the brothers were embarrassed after this statement. Their friend stared at them shrewdly for a moment and then laughed — one of his rare "Rosmersholm" laughs, as the brothers had christened such a happening.

"So that's the game? Coming here to déjeuner! Miss June with him?" They blushed over the tops of their beards. Invern began grumbling.

"Oswald!" exclaimed the boys deprecatingly; they were fond of him, notwithstanding his frowns and gloomy moods. A waiter was summoned and the order given for the mid-day meal. "Five plates, Louis, and have the whitest table linen in the house, please!"

After the introductions Oswald again admired the girl he had seen the previous night. She had accompanied the fraternal pair much against the wish of her guardian to a ball in the Quarter and she had not, she said, found it wonderfully diverting. The color of her eyes was hazel — they were wide with golden flecks in them, the same curious gold as her hair — and her little ears and nose with its tiny nostrils, that became inflated when she was interested, held the gaze of the young man. Under his dyed eyebrows Count Van Zorn regarded the company. It was not quite to his liking, the Hollin brothers soon discovered, so they

THE SUPREME SIN

engaged him in conversation and paid him exaggerated compliments. His bird-like profile, with the dull, prominent eyes, moved slowly from one brother to the other.

"Who's your friend?" he finally asked. He was told all sorts of impossible things; Invern was the coming composer; he had not arrived yet, but —! The Count grunted. He had heard this blague before. In Paris all your artistic friends are just about to, but never do, arrive. Miss Tilney spoke to Invern.

"It is charming to think of an American giving up his great country for the sake of music — preferring notes to gold." He made a gesture of disapproval.

"Ah, don't play the modest genius," she gayly cried. "You know, I am very sensitive to genius. I've never heard your music, yet I'm sure you are doomed to greatness — or sorrow." She added these last two words under her breath. Oswald heard them. He started and looked into her eyes, but he might as well have questioned two pools of light; they reflected no sentiment, nor did they directly return his glance. Across the table the Count made a motion and she colored; he summoned at the same time the attention of the young composer.

"You write music, do you?" he asked in a grating voice. "I am a composer myself. I studied with a great Russian musician, now dead. I——"

"Tell us about *Sar* Merodack Péladan," interrupted the vivacious Willy; "tell us if you ever witnessed his incantations." Every one but the Count and Invern laughed. The girl rapidly said something to her guardian. It must have been in Russian. He shook his head.

"Not to-day," he answered in French.

"No secrets!" the brothers adjured. At last the crowd began to modulate into that hazy amiable humor which follows a copious breakfast. As they drank coffee conversational themes were preluded, few developed; the ball of dialogue was lightly tossed and Oswald noticed that Miss Tilney could, at will, be American, French, German, Russian, and English, and again Russian. Like a many-colored skein she unwound her various temperaments according to her mood. With him she was sombre; once she flashed anger at the Count and showed her teeth; for the two Hollins she played any tune they wished. The real June Tilney — what was she? Oswald wondered. But, when he fancied himself near the edge of a revelation, his mind must have collided with her guardian's — Van Zorn's expression was repellent. Invern greatly disliked him. The talk drifted to art, thence to religion, and one of the Hollins jested about the Devil. Count Van Zorn fixed him at once.

"No one must mock sacred things in my presence," he coldly announced. The others were startled.

"M. Van Zorn!" said Miss Tilney. Oswald

saw her hands fluttering in nervous excitement.

"I mean it," was the firm response of the Count. "The Devil is the mainspring of our moral system. Mock him and you mock God — who created him. Without him this world would be all light without shadow, and there would be no art, no music — the Devil is the greatest of all musicians. He created the chromatic scale — that's why Richard Wagner admired the Devil in music — what is Parsifal but a version of the Black Mass! Ah! it is easy to see that Wagner knew Baudelaire only too well in Paris, and was initiated into the mysteries of Satanism by that poet who wrote a Litany to Lucifer, you know, with its diabolic refrain!" These words were fairly pelted upon the eardrums of his listeners. The girl held her peace, the brothers roared at the joke, but Invern took the phrases as a serious insult. He arose and bowed.

"The Count sees fit to insult my art — very well! But I am not compelled to hear any more." Before he could leave June plucked at his sleeve and tried to hold him; stranger still was the behavior of the old man. He reached across the table, his hands clasped in supplication.

"My dear young man," he panted, "I meant no offense. Pray be seated. I adore your art and practise it daily. I am a devout Wagnerian. I was but repeating the wisdom of certain ancient Fathers of the Church who ascribed, not without cause, the origin of music to Satan. Do not be annoyed. Beg of him, June, not to go." Invern fell back in his seat bewildered by this brusque cannonade. The Count held up his ten skinny fingers.

"These claws," he cried, "are worn to the bone on the keyboard. I belong to an antique generation, for I mingle music and magic. Credit me with good intentions. Better still, visit me soon — to-night — June, we go nowhere to-night, hein! Perhaps as you do not believe in the existence of the Devil, perhaps music — *my music* — may —— "

Oswald received a shock, for a small foot was placed upon his and pressed down with such electric vigor that he almost cried aloud. It told him, this foot, as plainly as if its owner had spoken: "Say no! Say no!" Responding to a stronger will than his own, he did not answer.

"Ha, you fear the Devil! But I assure you the Devil is a gentleman. I have met him, conversed with him." His voice filed down to a brittle whisper and to the acute perception of the young man an air of melancholy enveloped the speaker. Oswald hung his head, wondering all the while. Was this fanatic really in his sane senses? And the girl — what part did she play in such a life? Her voice cut sharply across his perplexity.

"Dear guardian, stop your Devil talk. I'm sick of it. You spoil our fun. Besides, you

THE SUPREME SIN

know the Devil is not a gentleman at all — the Devil is a woman." Shocked at the very tone of her voice, almost as harsh and guttural as her uncle's, Oswald intercepted a look rapidly exchanged between the Count and his ward. The blood rushed to his head and he slowly balled his fists. Then he arose:

"I don't know what you boys expect to do to-night, but I'm going to see the Devil — I mean the Count; that is, if he does not withdraw his invitation." The Hollins looked regretfully at Oswald and Miss Tilney. She had upset the salt and was slowly passing the tips of her fingers over its gritty surface, apparently dreaming, leagues distant. The Count was almost amiable.

"Ah, my dear June, I shall at last have an auditor for my bad Wagner playing! I live, Monsieur Invern, around the corner in the little Impasse du Maine, off the Avenue. We are neighbors, I think, and perhaps it may interest you to know that we, June and myself, inhabit the old atelier of Bastien Lepage, where he painted Sarah Bernhardt, where, also, unfortunate Marie Bashkirtseff was often wheeled to see the dying painter."

"Oh! oh!" remonstrated the girl in a toneless voice, "first Devil-worship, and now studio scandal. Fie!" Her high spirits had vanished; her face was ash-grey as she bowed to Invern. After shaking hands with the brothers, Count Van Zorn turned to him and said:

"Don't forget—eleven o'clock. Impasse du

Maine. The Devil perhaps; anyhow, Wagner. And the Devil is a gentleman." He tittered, baring his gums, his painted eyebrows high on his forehead.

"The Devil is a woman," tremulously insisted the girl. "Have you forgotten Klingsor and his 'Rose of Hell'?" With Van Zorn she disappeared.

II

When he reached his room Invern sat on the bed. These new people puzzled him. He had shaken off the Hollin brothers, telling them they were idiots to have introduced such an old lunatic to him.

"But we thought you liked occult Johnnies!" had been their doleful answer; and then Oswald bade them seek the old Nick himself, but leave him to his own thoughts; many had clustered about his consciousness during that afternoon; the principal one, the girl. Who was she? With all the boastings of the brothers that Count Van Zorn was welcome in distinguished musical circles, Oswald made up his mind to a decided negative. That man never went into the polite world nowadays, though he may have done so years before. An undefinable atmosphere of caducity and malodorous gentility clung to this disciple of music and the arts esoteric. How came it then that June Tilney, so mundane, so charming, so youthfully alert, could tolerate the vulture? What a vulture's glance suggest-

THE SUPREME SIN

ing inexpressible horrors was his brief, warning look! Oswald grew dizzy. "By God!" he groaned, "no, not that! But surely some sort of diabolic business!"

Why not go? Nothing but boredom could result at the worst, and boredom in his life was rapidly merging into a contempt for existence, contempt for this damnable Parisian morass. His ambition had winged away years before. Occasionally at dusk, on white summer nights, he seemed to discern a flash of some shining substance aloft, and felt his eyes fill, while in his ears he heard the humming of a great colored melody. Then he would make marks in his note-book and the next day forget his infrequent visitor; he believed in old-fashioned inspiration, but when it did arrive he was too indifferent to open the doors of his heart.

The Devil? Any belief but the dull, cynical unfaith of his existence, any conviction, even a wicked one, any act of the will, rather than the motiveless, stagnant days he was leading. Why not call on the Count? Why not see June Tilney again? He recalled vaguely the freshness of her face, of her presence. Yes, alert was the word, alert, as if she were guarding herself against an enemy. Ah! hiding a secret. *That* was in her light fencing, feathery raillery, cold despondency, half-smothered anger, fierce outburst, and, at the close, in her obstinate reiteration. What did it all mean? He sat on his bed and wondered.

BEDOUINS

And in the dim light of early evening he heard his name called, once, twice — with the memory of June Tilney's warning earlier in the day pressing thick upon his spirit, he rushed into the hallway from whose vacancy came no response to his excited challenge. Yet he could have sworn to the voice, a soundless voice which had said to him: "Don't go! Don't go!" Oswald put on his hat, picked up his walking-stick, and left the house. . . .

III

He wandered up and down the Boul' Mich' obsessed by his ideas, and the clocks in the cafés were pointing to five minutes of eleven when he turned from the Avenue du Maine into the little street, closed at one end, which bears the name of the adjacent avenue. Invern had never been before in this Impasse du Maine, though he had passed it daily for ten years. He remembered it as a place where painters and sculptors resided; it was dark, and the buildings for the most part were dingy, yet his impression, as he slowly moved along the lower side of the street, was not a depressing one. He reached the number given him as the bells in the neighboring church began to sound the hour. He had not time to summon the concierge when a hand was laid upon his arm; a woman, wearing a hood, and enveloped in a long cloak, peered at him through a heavy veil. He knew that it was June

THE SUPREME SIN

Tilney and his heart began to pump up the blood into his temples. She stooped as if endeavoring to hide her identity, and in her hand she carried a little cane.

"Don't go in!" she adjured the young man who, astounded by this apparition, regarded her with open-mouthed disquiet.

"Don't go in — there!" she again admonished him. "It means peril to your immortal soul if you do. I caution you for the *second* time."

"But how can it harm me?"

"I have warned you," she answered abruptly — was this his June Tilney of the bright morning airs? — "and I repeat: it is my wish that you do not visit there to-night." Something in her tone aroused opposition.

"Nevertheless, Miss Tilney, I mean to see the Devil to-night."

"Then go see her! But deny her if you dare!" She vanished in a doorway across the street. . . .

Shocked as was Oswald, he stolidly pulled the bell until the massive doors opened. A light at the end of a large, dim court showed him the staircase of the atelier. A moment later he had let fall a grinning bronze knocker in the image of a faun's hoof, and he had hardly time to ask himself the mystery of Miss Tilney's request, when he was welcomed by Count Van Zorn.

Nothing could have been pleasanter than the apartment into which he was conducted. The Count apologized for the absence of the young lady — Miss Tilney was a slave to social obligations! Invern winced. He looked about while the Count busied himself with carafe and glasses. Decidedly an ideal home for a modern wizard of culture. Book-shelves crowded with superb volumes, pictures of the Barbizon school on the walls, an old-fashioned grand pianoforte, an alcove across which was drawn black velvet drapery; everything signalized the retreat of a man devoted to literature and the arts. There were no enchantments lurking in the corners. Then his glance fell upon a warmly colored panel, a Monticelli, of luscious hues with richly wrought figures. It depicted a band of youths and maidens in flowing costumes, strayed revellers from some secret rites, but full of life's intoxication; hard-by stood an antique temple, at its portals a wicked smiling garden god. And over all was the flush of a setting sun, a vivid stain of pomegranate. . . . The desk of the piano held an engraving. Invern approached, but turned away his head. He saw that it was by that man of unholy genius, Félicien Rops. The Count crossed to his visitor and smilingly told him to look again.

"My Rops! You do not admire this Temptation of St. Anthony? No? Yet how different in conception from the conventional combination of the vulgar and voluptuous. Wagner's Parsifal is only a variation on this eternal theme of the Saint tempted by the Sinner. The Woman here is crucified — what a novel idea!"

THE SUPREME SIN

Invern was ill at ease. The place was not what it seemed. He read the titles of several imposing tomes: the Traité Methodique de Science Occulte, by Dr. Papus; Sar Péladan's Amphitheatre des Sciences Mortes, and Comment on devient mage; Au Seuil du Mystère and Le Serpent de la Genése, by Stanislaus de Guaita. Eliphas Levi, Nicolas Flamel, Ernest Bosc, Saint-Martin, Jules Bois, Nehor, Remy de Gourmont's Histoires Magiques, and many other mystics were represented. Upon the dados were stamped winged Assyrian bulls, the mystic rose, symbolic figures with the heads of women and anonymous beasts, lion's paws terminating in fish-tails and serpent scales. Inscriptions in a dead language, possibly Chaldean, streamed over the walls, and the constellations were painted in gold upon a dark-blue ceiling. Luini's Sacrifice to Pan, an etching of the picture in the Brera at Milan, caught his eye and he wondered why its obvious Satanic quality had been so seldom noted by diabolists. A cumbrous iron lamp of ornate Eastern workmanship, in which burned a wisp of green flame, comprised all that was bizarre in this apartment; otherwise, the broad student's table, the comfortable chairs and couches, did not differ from hundreds of other studios on the left bank of the Seine.

Count Van Zorn coaxed Invern into a lounging chair and gave him a glass of wine. It was Port, of a quality that to the young man's palate tasted like velvet fire. He was soon smoking a strong cigar in company with the old man, his fears quite obliterated. But his visitor noted that the Count was engrossed. As he sat, his eyes fastened upon the pattern of the polished parquet, Van Zorn looked like a man planning some grave project, perhaps a great crime. His head was hollowed at the temples, on his forehead the veins were puffy, his eyebrows, black as ink in the morning, were now interspersed with whitish-gray — the dye had worn away. At intervals he groaned snatches of melody, and once Invern heard him gabble in a strange tongue.

"And the music and the magic!" broke in the young man, weary of this interval. Slowly Van Zorn arose and stared at him steadily with his bird-of-prey eyes.

"Have you ever realized," he finally began in sing-song tones, "what an instrument for good or evil is the art you profess to practise? Hear me out," he continued, as the composer made a motion of dissent; "I don't refer to the facile criticism which classifies some music profane, some music sacred. The weaklings who are hurt by sensual operatic music would be equally hurt by a book or a picture; I refer to the music that is a bridge between here and — over there, over there!" His voice sank as he waved his lean brown fingers toward the alcove. "In the days of old, when man was nearer to nature, nearer to the gods, music was the key

THE SUPREME SIN

to all the mysteries. Pan and Syrinx answered its magic summons. A lost art, lost with the vulgarization of the other beautiful arts, you say? I deny it!" He drew up his rickety figure as if he held the keys of a conquered city.

"No! I repeat, music is still the precious art of arts and across its poisonous gulf of sound, on the other side, *over there*," — again he pointed to the alcove, with its sable velvet funeral pall — "the gods await our homage. Wagner — a worshipper at the diabolic shrine — pictured his faith in Parsifal. He is his own Klingsor, and the music he made for the evocation of Kundry came straight from the mouth of hell. Ah! how it burns the senses! How it bites the nerves'— 'Gundryggia there, Kundry here!' Yes, the gods and the greatest of all the gods, my master. Music is the unique spell that brings him to his worshippers on earth. We near the end of things. This planet has lived its appointed years. All the sins — *save the supreme one* — have been committed, all the virtues have bleached in vain our cowardly souls. Tell me, young man, tell me," he grasped Oswald by his wrist, "do you long for a sight of the true master? Through the gates of music will you go with me to *my* heaven where dwells the Only One?"

Invern nodded. He was more curious than afraid. With apish agility Van Zorn darted to the pianoforte and literally threw his hands upon its keyboard. A shrill dissonance in B minor sounded; like the lash of hail in his face the solitary auditor felt the stormy magnetism of the playing. He had sufficient control of his critical faculties — though it seemed as if he were launched into space on the tail of some comet — to realize the desperate quality of the performance. It was not that of a virtuoso; rather the travail of a spirit harshly expressing itself in a language foreign to its nature. The symmetry of the Wagner structure was almost destroyed; yet between the bits of broken bars and splintered tones there emerged the music of some one else, a stranger, newer Wagner. Was the Horla of Wagner buried in this demoniacal prelude to the second act of Parsifal struggling into palpable being! Carried before the banners of this surging army of tones, Oswald clutched his couch and eagerly listened to the evil music of Kundry and Klingsor.

He saw the stony laboratory with its gloomy battlements, from which the necromancer Klingsor witnessed Parsifal defeat the emasculate squires. He saw the mystic abyss hidden in the haze of violet vapor whence, obeying the hoarse summons of her master, Kundry slowly emerged. Her scream, the symphonic scream of woman, beast, or devil, fell upon his ears as though an eternity of damned souls had gnashed their teeth. And the echoes of her laughter reverberated through the porches of hell.

Gundryggia dort! Kundry hier! The succubus, or she-devil, demon, Rose of Hell, after

THE SUPREME SIN

vainly refusing to obey the demands of the harsh magician, sank with a baffled cry: "Oh! Woe is me!" The vast fabric of Klingsor's abode shivered, dissipated into nothingness. But there followed no shining garden filled with strange and gorgeous flowers, shapes of delights, wooing maidens with promises of unearthly love on their lips. Vainly Oswald awaited that scene of tropical splendor with its dream-terraces, living arabesques, and harmonious comminglement of sky and mountain, earth and fountain, the fair mirage painted by Klingsor's dark art. It did not appear. Instead the music became no longer Wagner's, became no longer music. Van Zorn amid brazen thunders wrenched himself from the keyboard, and prostrate upon the floor fairly kissed its surface, mumbling an awful litany. The room was murky, though violet hues suffused the velvet at the end. Invern became conscious of a third person, where he could not say. An icy vibration like the remote buzzing of monstrous dynamos apprised him that a door or window had been opened in the apartment which permitted the entrance of — what! His heart beat in the same rhythm with the mighty dynamos and the hoarse chanting of the Count.

"O Exiled Prince on whom was wrought such wrong!
 Who, conquered, still art impious and strong!"
"O Satan have mercy on us!"
"O Satan, patron saint of evil!"
"O Satan take pity on our misery!"

BEDOUINS

"O Prince of Suicide, Maker of music!"
"O Satan have pity on us!"
*"O Father of Pain, King of Desolation, true Master of
    the House of Planets!"*
"O Satan have mercy on us!"
"O Creator of black despair!"
"O Satan take pity on us!"

Indifferent Christian as was Invern, his knees knocked at this sacrilegious Baudelairian invocation. The violet grew in intensity as the prayers of the blasphemer increased. Slowly across the sombre velvet stretched in patibulary attitude a human skeleton. No thorns crowned its grinning skull; instead a live viper wreathed about its bony nest and turned glittering eyes upon the two men. Van Zorn's voice became a wail, calling down imprecations on earth to men of good-will. He cursed life and praised death, and his refrain was ever:

"O Satan, take pity on our misery!"

Oswald no longer heard him. With hysterical agitation he remarked the transformation of the adumbrated phantom. The skeleton had begun to carnify — its frame was first covered with ivory-white flesh, and then, with amazing velocity, a woman bourgeoned before his eyes. Gone the skull, gone the viper. In their stead emerged the delicate head of a goddess — filleted by Easter lilies — with smiling lips, enticing pose, the figure of a delicious nubility. Hazel were the wide, gold-flecked eyes that

THE SUPREME SIN

shot forthright shafts into the bosom of Oswald, and charged him with ineffable longing. The arms, exquisite in proportion, the graciously modelled torso, pierced him with an epileptic ecstasy. And the crazy tones of Van Zorn assailed his ears as if from a great distance:

"O Satan, have mercy on us!"

But the entranced youth cared little now for the diabolic litany. One idea seized and was burning up the vital spark of him. As the creature waxed in beauty he knew her — June Tilney! Yes, it was she — or was it the daughter of the devil in the Rops picture? — who drew him toward her with an irresistible caress in her eyes; eyes full of the glamour of Gehenna, eyes charged with sins without joy, penitence without hope. Forgotten her warnings before this Kundry of Golgotha.

"*O Satan come down to us*," rhythmically crooned the grovelling old man.

This, Satan? This radiant maiden with the flowery nimbus and beaming eyes, her young breasts carolling a magnificat as they pointed to the zenith — Oswald stumbled to the foot of the gibbet, in his ears the throbbing of death. Her glance of cadent glory transfixed him. Scorched by the vision, some fibre snapped in his brain and he triumphantly cried:

"Thou art a goddess, not the Devil."

A freezing blast overturned him, the saints of

hell encircled him, as he heard Van Zorn's grinding sobs:

"Thou hast denied the Devil! Thou hast committed the Supreme Sin! Quickly worship, else be banished forever from the only Paradise!"

Sick, his lips twisting with anguish, Invern had sufficient will to close his eyes and despairingly groan: "Son of Mary, save me!" The apparition crumbled. After a panic plunge he found himself somehow in the wintry street, his forehead wet with fear, his nerves tugging in their sheaths like wild animals leashed, his heart a cinder in a world of smoke. . . .

From Asia Minor, years later, the brothers received a letter signed by Oswald Invern. In it there were misty hints of monastic immurement, and the hopelessness of expiating a certain strange crime, compared with which the sin against the Holy Ghost is but a youthful peccadillo. The Hollin boys giggled in unison.

"What joy!" they exclaimed, "to have invented the Supreme Sin!"

II
BROTHERS-IN-LAW

WITH the vision of an antique marble façade lingering in his memory he slowly walked up the Avenue, only stopping at Fiftieth Street to turn and as leisurely retrace his route. Vincent Serle was in the middle of his vigorous life, but this day, an early one in April, his forces seemed arrested; like the curling wave which crests before its ultimate recoil and crumble. He attributed his mood to the weather. It was not precisely spring-fever, but a general slackening of physical fibre. He felt almost immoral: he desired respite from toil; he longed for some place where his eyes would not encounter palette or print; and, a versatile man of uncertain purpose, he longed to write a novel, chiefly about himself.

The clock on the church-tower told him that he was farther down-town than he had planned. He had mechanically spoken to passing acquaintances. He had saluted Mrs. Larce, over whose portrait he was laboring, with a vacant regard and flamboyant hat. Then he emerged from his engulfing spleen and hastily ascended Delmonico's steps. It was his day of disappointments. All the windows in the café were occupied; nothing remained except a large table in the centre of the room, decidedly an unpleasant spot, with people passing and repassing. He hesitated and would have gone away when he remembered that this hour always saw a mob of hungry folk at any establishment. And Benedict, his favorite waiter, whispered to him that he would assiduously attend to monsieur's wants. The bored painter sank heavily into his chair.

The meal was not an enlivening one. Like most artists educated in Paris, Vincent never took anything save coffee and rolls before one o'clock. He was not an early riser; he deplored morning work, being lazy and indifferent; but he soon discovered that if he were to keep pace with the desperate pace of New York artistic life he dared not waste the first half of the day. Mrs. Larce, for example, insisted upon a ten-o'clock sitting. At that precise hour he wished himself a writer with liberty to work at midnight; then he might indulge in more tobacco, dreams, and later uprisings. In the meantime he was munching his fish without noting its flavor, a fact that Benedict witnessed with disappointed eyes.

He had achieved coffee and cognac and was about to light a black cigar when a man hurried in, and, after gazing at the coveted window-tables, sat himself opposite Serle with a short nod, though hardly looking at him. The match burned Serle's fingers and he struck a fresh one. Instinctively he stood up, searching the room for another place. The garçon asked if he desired his account. Vincent shook his head and fumingly demanded a newspaper; behind it he swallowed his brandy and puffed his cigar. The fine print melted into a blurred mass before his eyes and his hands trembled. He could feel the beating of blood at his wrists and temple. He did not peep over the paper rampart because of his discomposed features.

"Damn him!" he thought, "I wonder if he knows me yet?"

The newcomer calmly ate his omelette with the air of a man intent upon some problem. He was not so tall, so dark as Serle, but older, wirier and of a type familiar to Fifth Avenue after four o'clock on fine afternoons: — a lawyer, broker, an insurance officer, but never an artist. He did not glance at his table companion until the other had folded his newspaper, and then without a gleam of recognition.

"He doesn't know me," reflected Serle; "so much the better, I'll not go away. I'll watch him. It will be interesting."

He sardonically hoped that the absorbed man would choke as he swallowed his chop. Then he smiled at his vindictive temper, smiled bitterly because of his childishness — after all the fellow was not to blame; he had been a mere accomplice of a stronger, a more unprincipled will. Yet, slowly studying the face, he could not call it a foolish one. Its owner showed by his concentrated pose, the stern expression of his mask, that he was not a weakling.

"But," mused the painter, "I've seen men with jaws as if modelled in granite, eyes that imperiously reminded you that they were your master, men whose bearing recalled that of a triumphant gladiator; well, these same individuals, artists, despots, brutes, bankers, were like whipped dogs in the presence of some woman. No. Hector Marden's outward semblance is not an indication of the real man. We are all consummate actors in our daily lives, none more so than those who have much to conceal."

Hector Marden — and had he not much to conceal — the beast! Vincent's clinched fists were drumming on the table. "Come," he pondered, "I'll have to cease this baby game or I'll end by making a scene and consequently an ass of myself." He stared at Benedict just as Marden raised his finger. The waiter hurried to the table and presented his memoranda to the men. Serle frowned. He was in a nasty humor.

"What's this, Benedict?" He tendered the embarrassed garçon his slip of paper.

"Pardon, a thousand times pardon, monsieur! I made a mistake." Marden looked up smiling.

"I fear I have the bill intended for you," he said, in a conciliating tone.

"It's nothing," murmured Serle. Both men bowed. The accounts were soon settled and

BROTHERS-IN-LAW

Benedict nervously retreated to the background. But neither one stirred. Vincent, without pausing to analyze his action, offered Marden the newspaper. It was politely refused. Possibly because of the mellowness of the moment, or the ample repose that follows luncheon, Marden was not averse from entering into conversation, one of hazy indirectness, equally suggestive and non-committal. He made a few commonplace remarks about the unseasonable heat, the deplorable twilight of New York's tower-begirt highways, and soon, against the prompting of his inner spirit, Serle chimed an accordance. They chatted. Benedict discreetly moved nearer. Presently Serle asked his neighbor if he would have a cigar or perhaps a liqueur.

"I don't mind," rejoined Marden. "The fact is I feel lazy this afternoon. I had expected to meet a friend here — a client of mine — but I fancy he is off somewhere wondering if New York shall ever boast a decent sky-line. He is an architect and enthusiastic over French Gothic." Serle's ears began to burn.

"Architecture in New York? That's a tall joke. Curiously enough, though, this very morning I was admiring the new library. It has a stunning façade. If I were Emperor of America I'd raze every building within the radius of ten blocks so as to give the building a chance. Only think of the Cathedral without a house near it!"

"You are an artist, evidently," Marden said

without the faintest trace of curiosity in his voice. Serle nodded. Benedict with clasped hands hinted that the two gentlemen might prefer a window. There were empty tables upon which the sun no longer shone, since the formidable walls across the street blocked its rays. The painter shuddered. They would surely be seen by impertinent passers-by. He sent the man away, sharply adding that he would be called when needed. As for Marden, he was languidly drifting on the current of his fancy. Was it pleasant or unpleasant? The watcher could not decide. But he had made up his mind that he would draw Marden up to the danger-line, and if discovered, if discovered? He would at least tell him what he thought of the mean scoundrel who had ——

"I've noticed," Marden broke in on Serle's ugly revery, "that painters seem to have lots of time on their hands. I beg your pardon. You have quite as much reason for advancing a similar remark about a professional man. Here I am lounging as if I had no office or desk loaded with unanswered correspondence. But I assure you I don't often dissipate this way, and I take it you are of the same opinion regarding yourself." He paused.

"You spoke of painters loafing. What made you single out that particular profession? I believe it may be called a profession," Vincent laughed.

"Oh! You said you were a painter —— "

"Yes, but you were not thinking of me, I'll wager. You've only seen me half an hour."

"You're right; I was not thinking of painters, or of you in general, but of a particular case that came under my personal observation."

"Yes, yes," eagerly responded Serle, as he mentally abused the lawyer for his measured, pedantic delivery. "Your story interests."

Marden glanced at the other's flaming cheeks and replied, rather abruptly:

"But you haven't heard it yet. However, it's not much of a yarn. It happened — several years ago. A lady, a client, came to me for advice. She was married, married, I say, to an artist, a painter — a big, good-for-nothing fellow, who was lazy, who drank, ran after his models and spent her money." Marden was interrupted.

"Excuse me, you said the lady was rich?"

"Did I?"

"Certainly, spent her money was your last phrase."

"Oh! — Well, perhaps I shouldn't have said her money. She had no money. I meant that her husband had money and didn't spend it on her. A mere slip of the tongue."

"Good. I'm a regular cross-examiner, you see."

"True. You might prove a difficult witness in the chair. My friend—my client, informed me that her husband was so lazy that he remained in bed until one or two o'clock in the afternoon; then he would slowly dress and saunter for a walk, and often she did not see him until the next morning."

"How did he make a living?"

"Oh, I suppose he painted a portrait or two and managed to get on."

"A portrait or two? That would hardly pay household expenses — that is, unless your friend — I mean your client's husband, was a Sargent or a Boldini. Then they could have struggled along at the rate of one portrait every year." Serle laughed so harshly that Marden looked at him wonderingly.

"I see you are acquainted with the artistic temperament, as they call it in the newspapers," observed the lawyer.

"Not as they call it, but as it is. My dear sir, an artist is not built to put in a ton of coal every day. A man whose brain is delicately adjusted, whose whole soul is in his eyes ——"

"When he sees a pretty girl?" The sly tone of Marden angered the painter.

"No, hang it! For a painter there are no pretty, no ugly girls; no pretty, no ugly landscapes; no agreeable, no disagreeable subjects. Only a surface to be transferred to canvas, to be truthfully rendered. And that's what business men, with their lack of imagination, will never understand." He spoke hotly.

"I confess I have a lack of imagination when it comes to an appreciation of the artistic temperament." Marden said this so slyly that Serle at once begged his pardon.

"After all, we are not at Delmonico's just to thrash out a stale question. Pray go on — your story interests me strangely."

"It's not very interesting — that's all I know. The woman left the man ——"

"For another?" calmly interjected Vincent.

"Not at all, not at all — that is, not at the time." The lawyer fumbled his glass, his expression overcast.

"You know what strange creatures women are. I had the greatest difficulty in persuading my client to make up her mind. She suffered, yet she cared for the fellow ——"

Serle impatiently asked: "But you haven't revealed what the fellow did to her — what his special crime! Didn't he give her a good home?"

"My dear sir! A good home when he turned night into day! A good home when he seldom put brush to canvas! A good home — why, I thought I told you he was too friendly with his models."

"His models! A portraitist! Do you mean his sitters? Did he flirt with them? If he did so he was a fool, for he was killing the goose that laid the — No, I'll not be so impolite. I meant to say he would endanger his reputation." Marden dryly laughed.

"That's good — reputation is good. My client informed me, and she is a serious woman, that she never met an artist who could be relied upon. And she knew, for she was one herself."

Serle's jaw dropped. "How odd! What did she do?"

"Oh, she painted a little, just enough to make pin-money and to annoy her husband. You see, it was this way. She did not care to take money from a man she loathed."

"Loathed!"

"I said — loathed. She literally loathed him. She told me so."

"Why didn't she leave him sooner? Besides, a few moments ago you said he never offered her money. Now, she loathed him so she wouldn't take any——"

"Ah! That's not in my fable," tartly answered Marden. Again he turned gloomy and tapped nervously on the table.

The afternoon waned. A soft light slipped through the high curtained windows and modulated into glancing semitones over the richly decorated apartment. Several men entered — the vanguard of the five-o'clock brigade of absintheurs. Serle became nervous. What if! — But he determined to take the chance of seeing some imbecile who might salute him by name. He leaned forward on his folded arms and asked with a show of concern:

"And what became of your charming client?"

"My charming — Oh! Why, she married and settled down."

"At last! Is she happy?"

BROTHERS-IN-LAW

"How can I tell?" The response betrayed an irritable nuance.

"I didn't mean to put the question so bluntly. The reason I ask is a simple one. I studied a case not unlike the one you narrated. It is just as sordid and commonplace. My artist, also a painter, had married a pupil whom he taught — as much as she could absorb. She hadn't much talent; it was the sort you see expressed on fans and bon-bon boxes.

"She might have been all right if her admiring friends had not told her that she had more talent than her husband — really, there wasn't enough between them both to set the river on fire. However, she devilled him so effectually that he took a separate studio to get away from the sound of her voice and from their home. Like your painter, he turned day into night, but with a difference; he made illustrations for the magazines and newspapers, painted cheap portraits, demeaned himself generally to get money enough to run the house. She enjoyed herself, flirted, went into society of some sort, a cheap compromise between Bohemia and the frayed fringe of Fifth Avenue — you may not know the variety, as you are a member of another profession. It is diverting, this society, because it is as false as the hair on the head of its women. The bohemian side largely consists of bad claret, worse music, and ghastly studio teas; its fashionable side, poverty-stricken grand ladies with tarnished reputations. I've seen it all. One of the sights of greater Gotham is this glittering set of fakirs. The woman I speak of was whirled off her feet by the cheap show. She was a fresh, pretty little girl when she came here from a small town up State. Her friends were ambitious fools, she was green — and very vain. So vain! Then her name crept into the newspapers; it's hard work keeping out of them nowadays. She was called 'The beautiful Mrs. Somebody, who painted exquisite miniatures of socially prominent ladies'; you know the style of such rot? The horror of it! Rather you don't, for you have never lived in this particular set —— "

"But, I do, I do!" cried Marden. "My client told me something of it." Serle sneered.

"She didn't tell you much or you might have asked her whether there wasn't another side to her case. The girl I am talking about went the pace; and, as an old philosopher on the police force remarks: 'When a woman is heading for hell, don't try to stop her; it's a waste of time.' Her husband saw it and he did try. Her friends knew it and helped her on her merry way. The painter even sent her to Europe, and with her some of her friends to keep her company, if they couldn't keep her straight. Well — Paris is worse than poison for such women. She was soon back in New York, leaving behind her a sweet record, many unpaid bills and with a half a dozen fools, picked up, God knows where, at her heels. And then he went away. It was too much. However, being a woman, she won all the sympathy. Her story was believed, not his, and —— "

"Singular coincidence. But wasn't the husband to blame a little?"

"Oh!" said Vincent. "Men are always to blame."

"Could he have forgiven her?"

"He did better, he forgot her."

"Did she go to the bad?" sympathetically inquired Marden.

"On the contrary. She married well — a professional man of some sort." He smiled with good-humored malice.

"And is she — is she — right now? I mean is she happy?"

"She will be happy always, a selfish little soul. You mean is her present husband happy?"

"Yes." Marden leaned back nonchalantly and his hands, lean-fingered, traversed the corner of the table. To Serle the air became as dense as a vapor-bath. He continued, mercilessly:

"Of course he is happy — her husband. Why shouldn't he be? He doesn't know."

"Doesn't know what? Really, you set me on edge," exclaimed Marden. He tried to smile, but his upper lip lifted, displaying white eye-teeth. Vincent lighted a fresh cigar. His arm did not tremble now. Then, swallowing the last of his cold coffee, he continued:

"Her husband doesn't dream the truth of her

life in New York and Paris. She is, as I said, very pretty and can pull the wool over any man's eyes. She is so interesting, so poetic, you know. She plays that little trick of the abused wife with the artistic temperament; plays it off on all the men she meets, on my friends —— "

"Your friends?"

"My friends know her as a capricious vixen, masquerading as a delicate oversoul. I knew her once." (Serle was cool; he had himself well in hand.) "And she always wins and still plays the game. At this moment she is probably fooling her husband, taking tea with some softhead. She gets her wealthy male friends —— "

"How does she get them? Tell me." Marden's voice was subdued. "Does she say to her husband that she must secure orders for miniatures by dining with rich fellows? Doesn't she —— "

"Really, my dear sir, I don't know everything about this clever lady's method. You seem quite taken with her story. It is, I pride myself, more exciting than your narrative of the artistic temperament." Vincent's intonations were markedly sarcastic. The older man's face was afire.

"Who the devil —— "

Benedict came to the table and placatingly asked:

"Is this Mr. Marden?"

"I'm Mr. Marden. What do you want?"

"Madame, your wife, has just arrived. She

BROTHERS-IN-LAW

is in the large salon with a gentleman, and she desires me to ask you to join her." The men arose.

"It was quite a pleasant afternoon, was it not?" In his most charming manner Serle put out his hand and Marden took it, grudgingly, his shrewd face surly, his little eyes suspiciously fastened on the smiling countenance of his companion. Then he followed the obsequious garçon, and Serle went into the street, first looking after the pair. He discerned Marden at a table on the Fifth Avenue side; with him was a fresh-colored, graceful woman, in elaborate afternoon toilette; a big, overdressed man sat beside her.

Once in a taxi Vincent Serle gave the order to cross over to Madison Avenue.

"I'll not risk passing that window," he muttered. "It was a mean trick, but it served the meddling fool right. I wonder which one of us lied the more? And I never saw Amy look so bewitching!"

III

GRINDSTONES

> "Yet each man kills the thing he loves,
>   By each let this be heard;
> Some do it with a bitter look,
>   Some with a flattering word.
> The coward does it with a kiss,
>   The brave man with a sword."
> —*Oscar Wilde.*

It was nearly nine o'clock in the evening when the young ladies entered the fashionable boarding-house drawing-room. Madame Recamier's, on the upper West Side, was large enough to defy the heated spell; yet the group seemed languid on this tepid night in June, fluttered fans and were not disposed to chatter. No one had called. Miss Anstruther, a brilliant brunette, cried out:

"Oh, my kingdom for a man!" Mild laughter was heard. The girl went to the grand piano and said: "What shall it be?"

"No Chopin," exclaimed Miss Beeslay.

"Do play a Chopin nocturne. Why, it's the very night for nocturnes. There's thunder in the air," protested Miss Pickett.

"Listen to Anne. Isn't she poetic—" By this time the young women were quite animated. Tea served, Madame Recamier sent down word by the black page to ask Miss Anstruther for a little music. The dark girl pouted, yawned, and finally began the nocturne in F minor. Before she had played two bars the door-bell rang, and its echoes were not stilled before a silvery gong sounded somewhere in the rear. The drawing-room was instantly deserted.

Presently the page brought in two young men, both in evening dress.

"We should like to see Miss Anstruther and Miss Pickett," said the delicate-looking fellow. "Say that Mr. Harold and a friend are here." The page departed. Mr. Harold and his companion paced the long apartment in a curious mood.

"Tea! They don't drink tea, do they?" asked the other man, a tall blond, who wore his hair like a pianist.

"I'm afraid that's all we'll get, Alfred; unless Madame Recamier comes down-stairs or else is magnetized by your playing. She keeps a mighty particular boarding-house."

"For God's sake, Ned, don't ask me to touch a piano. I've only come with you because you've raved about this dark girl and her playing. There they are!" Two came in; introductions followed, and the conversation soon became lively.

"We drink tea," said Anne Pickett, "because Madame Recamier believes it is good for the complexion."

BEDOUINS

"You have a hygiene like a young misses' school, haven't you?" said Ned, while Harold, fascinated by the rather gloomy beauty of Miss Anstruther, watched closely and encouraged her talk. She had a square jaw; her cheek-bones were prominent. She was not pretty. The charm of her face — it was more compelling than charming — lay in her eyes and mouth. Brown, with a hazel nuance, the eyes emitted a light like a cat's in the dark. Her mouth was a contradiction of the jaw. The lips were full and indicated a rich, generous nature, but the mask was one of a Madonna — a Madonna who had forsaken heaven for earth. Harold found her extremely interesting.

"Of course, you are musical?" he asked.

"Yes; I studied at Stuttgart, and have regretted it all my life. I can never get rid of the technical stiffness."

"Play for me," he begged. But playing was not to the girl's disposition. Sultry was the night, and a few faint flashes of heat-lightning near the horizon told of a storm to come. Anne Pickett was laughing very loudly at her companion's remarks and did not appear to notice the pair. Several times, at the other end of the long drawing-room, eyes peeped in, and once the black page put his head in the door and coughed discreetly.

It seemed a dull hour at Madame Recamier's.

Suddenly Harold placed his hand on Miss Anstruther's and said: "Come to the piano,"

GRINDSTONES

and, as one hypnotized, she went with him. He lifted the fall-board, put back the lid, glanced carelessly at the maker's name, and fixed the seat for the young woman. Anne Pickett was watching him from the other side of the room.

"Who's your friend? He acts like a piano man. There were three here last night."

"H'sh!" said Ned, as the pianist struck a firm chord in C-sharp minor and then raced through the Fantaisie-Impromptu. The man beside her listened and watched rather cynically as her strong fingers unlaced the involved figures of the music. That he knew the work was evident. When she had finished he congratulated her on her touch, observing: "What a pity you don't cultivate your rhythms!" She started.

"You are a musician, then?" Before he could answer, the page came in and whispered in her ear: "Madame Recamier wants to know if the gentlemen will have some wine."

Miss Anstruther blushed, got up from the piano and walked toward the window. Harold followed her, and Miss Pickett called out: "Ned, we can have some champagne; old Mumsey says so."

When Harold reached the girl she was leaning out of the window regarding the western sky. Darkness was swallowing up the summer stars: he put his hand on her shoulder, for she was weeping silently, hopelessly.

"How can you stand it?" he murmured, and

the ring in his voice caused the girl to turn about and face him, her eyes blurred but full of resentment.

"Don't pity me — don't pity me; whatever you feel, don't pity me," she said in a low, choked voice.

"My dear Miss Anstruther, let me understand you. I admire you, but I don't see why I should pity you." Harold was puzzled.

"Anne, he doesn't know; Harold doesn't know," cried Miss Anstruther, and Anne laughed, when a sharp flash of lightning almost caused the page to drop the tray with the bottles and glasses.

It grew hot; the wine was nicely iced, so the four young people drank and were greatly refreshed. Madame Recamier was justly proud of her cellar. Anne pledged Ned, and Harold touched glasses with Miss Anstruther, while the first thunder boomed in the windows, and the other boarders out in the back conservatory shivered and thirsted.

Harold went to the piano. He felt wrought up in a singular manner. The electricity in the atmosphere, the spell of the dark woman's sad eyes, her harsh reproof and her undoubted musical temperament acted on him like a whiplash. He called the page and rambled over the keyboard. Miss Anstruther sat near the pianist. Soon the vague modulations resolved into a definite shape, and the march from the Fantaisie in F minor was heard. It took form, it leaped into rhythmical life, and when the rolling arpeggios were reached, a crash over the house caused Miss Pickett to scream, and then the page entered with a tray.

Harold stopped playing. Miss Anstruther, her low, broad brow dark with resentment, said something to the boy, who showed his gums and grinned. "It's de wine, missy," he said, and went out on ostentatious tiptoe. The group in the conservatory watched the comedy in the drawing-room with unrelaxed interest, though little Miss Belt declared the thunder made her so nervous that she was going to bed. Madame Recamier rang the gong twice, and a few minutes later a smell of cooking mounted from the area kitchen. Harold started afresh. The storm without modulated clamorously into the distance, and orange-colored lightning played in at the window as he reached the big theme of the bass. It was that wonderful melody in F minor which Beethoven might have been proud to pen, and was followed by the exquisite group of double notes, so fragrant, so tender, so uplifting, that Anne Pickett forgot her wine; and the other girl, her eyes blazing, her cheek-bones etched against the skin, sat and knotted her fingers and followed with dazed attention the dance of the atoms in her brain. She saw Harold watching her as she went to school; Harold peeping in at the lodge of her college; Harold waiting to waylay her when she left her father's house, and she saw Harold that terrible night! He had reached the meditation in B and her pulses slackened. After the crash of the storm, after the breathless rush of octaves, Miss Anstruther felt a stillness that did not come often into her life. The other pair were sitting very close, and the storm was growling a diminuendo in the east. Already a pungent and refreshing smell of earth that had been rained upon floated into the apartment, and Harold, his eyes fixed on hers, was rushing away with her soul on the broad torrent of Chopin's magic music. She was enthralled, she was hurt; her heart stuck against her ribs and it pained her to breathe. When the last harp-like figure had flattened her to the very wall, she sank back in her chair and closed her eyes.

"Ho, Margery, wake up; your wine's getting warm!" cried lively Anne Pickett as she sipped her glass, and Ned rang the bell for the page. Harold sat self-absorbed, his hands resting on the ivory keys. He divined that he had won the soul of the woman who sat near him, and he wondered. He looked at her face, a strong face, in repose with a few hard lines about the eyes and mouth. He gazed so earnestly that she opened her eyes, and catching his regard, blushed — blushed ever so lightly. But he saw it and wondered again. More wine came, but Miss Anstruther refused and so did Harold. By this time the other pair were jolly. Ned called out:

"Harold, play something lively. Wake up

the bones, old man! Your girl isn't getting gay." Harold looked at her, and she walked slowly toward the conservatory. Miss Pickett, crazy Anne, as they called her, went to the piano and dashed into a lively galop. Ned drank another glass of wine and began to dance from the end of the room to the piano.

"Come on, let's have a good racket!" he yelled, as the piano rattled off in rag-time while Miss Anstruther and Harold sat on near the conservatory. The whispering increased behind them, but the girl did not hear it. The music unlocked her heart, and her commonplace surroundings faded. If she had but met a man like him that other time! She realized his innate purity, his nobility of nature. Little wonder that his playing aroused her, made live anew the old pantomime of her life. She unconsciously placed in the foreground of her history the figure of the man beside her, yet she had never before seen him. It was wonderful, this spiritual rebirth. Only that morning she told the girls at breakfast she could never love again — she hated men and their ways. "They are animals, the best of them!" and Madame Recamier laughed the loudest.

Harold left her, took another glass of wine, and seeing Miss Pickett light a cigarette, asked permission to do the same.

"Can't I bring you another glass of wine?" Harold tenderly asked. The gang of girls in the conservatory nudged one another and stared with burning eyes at Miss Anstruther through the lattice. She gently shook her head, and again he saw her blush. She did not stir. He began the luscious nocturne in B — the Tuberose Nocturne, and Madame Recamier's gong sounded. The page entered and said:

"No more piano playing to-night. Madame wants to sleep."

Miss Anstruther started so angrily that there was a titter behind the lattice. But she did not notice it; her whole soul was bent on watching Harold. He spoke to Ned, and Miss Pickett's jarring laugh was heard.

Then he went over to her, and, sitting down beside her, leaned and touched her face with his finger. The girl grew white and she felt her heart beat. At the next word, the old, tired, cold look came back, and she faced him as she had first received him.

Then suddenly the laughter behind the lattice grew noisy. Anne Pickett screamed out:

"Another of Margery's dreams shattered!"

Ned laughed and rang for more wine.

As they came down the steps the next morning Harold said to Ned:

"My boy, there are worse crimes than murdering a woman."

"Oh, let's get a cocktail," croaked Ned.

IV

VENUS OR VALKYR?

PAUL GODARD found the ride between Nuremberg and Baireuth discomforting. The hot July breezes that blew into the first-class coupé of the train were almost breath-arresting; and Paul had left Stuttgart that morning in a savage mood. The slowness of the railway service irritated him, the faces of his travelling companions irritated him, and he had shocked an Englishman by remarking early in the afternoon:

"If the old engine doesn't run any faster than this we had better get out and walk, or — push."

The other simply peered at the speaker and then resumed Wolzogen's book on Leading-Motives.

Three Roumanian ladies laughed in oily Eastern accents. They understood English, and the sight of a human being, a strong young man, in a passion about such a little matter as European railroad punctuality struck them as ridiculous. So they laughed again and Paul finally joined in, for he was an American.

He had been rude, but he couldn't help it; besides, it looked as if they would reach Bai-

BEDOUINS

reuth too late for the opening performance, and his was the laughter of despair.

The youthful pilgrim journeying to Baireuth was born in New York. He had studied music like most young people in his country, and had begun with that camel, that musical beast of all burdens, the piano. This he practised most assiduously at intervals, because he really loved music; but college, lawn-tennis, golfing, dancing, and motor-boating had claims not easily put aside. Naturally, the piano suffered until Paul left college; then for want of something better to do he took lessons from Joseffy and edified that master by his spurts of industry. His club began to encroach on his attention, and again the piano was forgotten. Paul, whose parents were rich, was not a society butterfly, but his training, instincts, and associations forced him to regard a good dinner, a good tailor, and a racing motor-car as necessary to his existence. From his mother he inherited his love of music, and his father, dead many years, had bequeathed him a library; better still, a taste for reading.

An average cultivated American, intensely self-conscious, too self-conscious to show himself at his best, ashamed of his finer emotions, like most of his countrymen, and a trifle spoiled and shallow.

One day Edgar Saltus told Paul he should read Schopenhauer, and he at once ordered the two volumes of The World as Will and Rep-

VENUS OR VALKYR?

resentation. It was not difficult reading, because he had been in Professor Bowne's class at college and enjoyed the cracking of metaphysical nuts. He began to get side glimpses of Wagner's philosophy, but despite the wit of the German Diogenes his pessimism repelled him. He could not agree with Saltus's ingenious defense of pessimism in his two early books, and he looked about for diversion elsewhere. Walter Pater's silken chords, velvety verbal music, had seduced Paul from the astringencies of Herbert Spencer, and Chopin made moonlight for his soul on morbid nights.

Yet Paul, with his selfish, well-bred, easy life, had encountered no soul-racking convulsions; he had never been in love, therefore he played the nocturnes of Chopin in a very unconvincing manner.

He always declared that Poe was bilious, and this remark gained for him the reputation of wit and scholar among his club associates.

The Calumel Club is not given to velléités of speech. . . .

II

Then Paul Godard fell into the clutches of Richard Wagner and swallowed much of him.

Chopin seemed tiny, exotic, and feminine compared to the sirocco blasts of the Baireuth master. Paul was not too critical, and, like most Americans, he measured music by its immediate emotional result. The greater the assault upon the senses, the greater the music. The logic was inescapable.

Friedrich Nietzsche was the next milestone in Paul's mental journeyings. The attack on Wagner, the attack on the morals that made our state stable, the savage irony, sparkling wit, and brilliant onslaught on all the idols, filled the mind of the young man with joy. He dearly loved a row, and though he recognized Nordau's borrowed polemical plumage, he liked him because of his cockiness.

So he devoured Nietzsche, reckless of his logical inferences, reckless of the feelings of his poor mother, a most devoted Episcopalian of the High Church variety. Paul always pained her with his sudden somersaults, his amazing change of attitude, and, above all, his heartless contempt for her idols, the Church and good society. Society sufficed her soul hunger, and Paul's renunciation of Mozart and Donizetti — she simply loved Lucia — his sarcastic flouting of churchgoers and his refusal to range himself, were additional weeds of woe in her mourning life.

There was Edith Vicker; but Paul was such a hopeless case and wouldn't see that a nice, pretty, rich, moderately intelligent, well-reared young woman was slipping through his fingers. Mrs. Godard often sighed that winter in her sumptuous uptown apartment.

Nietzsche revealed new intellectual vistas for Paul and he actually became serious. The

VENUS OR VALKYR?

notion of regarding one's own personality as a possible work of art to be labored upon and polished to perfection's point, set him thinking hard. What had he done with his life? What wasted opportunities! He deserted his club and began piano-playing again, and when reproached by his friends for his fickleness he excused himself by quoting Nietzsche; a thinker, as well as a snake, must shed his skin once a year, else death. He also was ready with Emerson's phrase about fools being consistent, and felt altogether very fine, and superior to his fellow-beings. Nietzsche feeds the flame of one's vanity, and Paul was sure that he belonged to the quintessential band of elect souls that is making for the Uebermensch — the Superman!

He really was a nice, boyish lad, and he could never pass a pretty girl — whether a countess or a chambermaid — without making soft eyes at her. Paul was popular; and so the Roumanian ladies laughed at him admiringly. Paul had left his mother in Paris, the heat was too trying for travel, and he was close to Baireuth on this torrid summer day, one Sunday afternoon in July.

Yet another hour before him, he turned his critical attention to the laughing trio. One was a princess. She told Paul so, and spoke of the sultry diversions of Bucharest. The second was a fat singer, who startled the Englishman by inquiring if there wasn't a good coloratura part in Parsifal. If there were, she intended asking

BEDOUINS

Frau Cosima Wagner to let her sing it; but if there wasn't, she supposed she would have to be content with the Forest Bird; even Melba had been a Waldvogel, why couldn't she be one also?

Her sparkling eyes and mountain of flesh amused Paul exceedingly. He knew Heinrich Conried very well, and he told the singer that when Parsifal was sung next season at the Metropolitan Opera House he would speak to the impresario and get her the part of Kundry. It was for a lark-like voice, such as the lady said she possessed, and full of Bellinian fioritura.

As he gravely related these fables he was conscious of the penetrating gaze of the third woman. She was tall, frail-looking, with a dark skin, hair black and glossy, and she had the most melancholy eyes in the world. Paul returned her glance with discretion. His eyes were Irish blue-gray and full of the devil at times, and they could be very sympathetic and melting when he willed. The two young people examined each other with that calm regard which, as Schopenhauer declares, mars or makes the destiny of a new generation. But metaphysics and the biology of the sexes bothered not at all the youth and maiden. ·Paul admired the classic regularity of her nose and forehead, and wondered why her face seemed familiar. Her mouth was large, irregular, perverse. It suggested Marie Bashkirtseff's, and it was just as yearning and dissatisfied. Despite their sadness,

VENUS OR VALKYR?

fun lurked in the corners of her eyes, and he knew that she enjoyed his harmless hoax.

Then they both burst out laughing, and the princess said in a surprised voice:

"Helena, why do you laugh with the young American gentleman?"

She also mentioned a family name that caused the New Yorker to stare. What, was this girl with the determined chin and brows the identical one who almost set Russia quarrelling with another nation and upset the peace of Roumania? Yes, it was, and Paul no longer puzzled over her face. It had been common property of the photographers and newspaper illustrators a few years ago, and as he mentally indexed its features he almost said aloud that her curious beauty had never been even faintly reproduced.

His imagination was stirred; Roumania had always seemed so remote, and here was he, Paul Godard, a plain American citizen, face to face with the heroine of one of those mysterious Eastern intrigues in which kings, crowns, queens, and ladies-in-waiting were all delightfully mixed up. So he chatted with Helena about Wagner and Degeneracy, and discovered that she was an admirer of Ludwig of Bavaria, Nietzsche, Guy de Maupassant, Poe, Schumann, Chopin, Marie Bashkirtseff, and all the rest of the sick-brained people born during the sick-brained nineteenth century. She, too, had written a book, which was soon to appear. It was full of the Weltzchmerz of Schopenhauer and the bold upspringing individualism of Nietzsche. She had odd theories concerning the Ring of the Nibelungs, and had read Browning's Sordello. She told Paul that she found but one stumbling-block in Wagner. How, she asked gravely, with a slight blush — how could Parsifal become Lohengrin's father?

Paul said he didn't know. It must have occurred long after his experiences with Kundry and the Flower Girls, and perhaps it was a sort of ——

"Oh, no, M. Godard!" she quickly answered. "Not that. The swan died, you know; besides, Parsifal was always a Pure Fool." Paul suggested that it might have been another of the same name but of a different family. And then the conversation went to pieces, for the soprano called out:

"Voilà! Baireuth, the Wagner theatre!" and they all craned their necks to catch the first glimpse of that mystic edifice built on the hill, the new musical Pantheon, the new St. Peter's of the Bewitched Ones.

And the Englishman continued to calmly read about the Loki-motif as the train slowly steamed into Baireuth.

III

Paul found comfortable lodgings in the Lisztstrasse and his new friends went to the Hotel Sonne. At half-past four he was up on the hill looking at the world, and as immaculately dressed

VENUS OR VALKYR?

as if he stood in the bow window of the Calumel Club, ogling Fifth Avenue girls. He was only vaguely interested in the approaching performance, and his pulses did not quicken when Donner's motif told the gabbling, eager throng that the great Trilogy was about to unfold its fables of water, wood, and wind. He took his seat unconcernedly, and then the house became black and from space welled up those elemental sounds, not merely music, but the sighing, droning swish of waters. The Rhine calmly, majestically stole over Paul's senses, he forgot New York, and when the curtains parted he was with the Rhine Daughters, with Alberich, and his heart seemed to stop beating. All sense of identity vanished at a wave of Wagner's magic wand, and not being a music-critic, his ego was absorbed as by the shining mirror in the hand of a hypnotist. This, then, was Wagner, a Wagner who attacked simultaneously all the senses, vanquished the strongest brain, smothered, bruised, and smashed it; wept, sang, surged, roared, sighed in it; searched and ravished your soul until it was put to flight, routed, vanquished, and brought bleeding and captive to the feet of the master.

The eye was promise-crammed, the ears sealed with bliss, and Paul *felt* the wet of the waters. He panted as Alberich scaled the slimy steeps, and the curves, described by the three swimming mermaids, filled him with the joy of the dance.

The rape of the Rhinegold, the hoarse shout

BEDOUINS

of laughter from Alberich's love-forsworn lips, and the terrified cries of the three watchers were to Paul as real as Wall Street.

Walhall didn't bore him, and he began at last to catch faint clues of the meaning of the mighty epic. He went to the underworld, and saw the snake, the ring, and the tarnhelm; he heard the anvil chorus — so different from Verdi's! — he saw the giants quarrelling over their booty, and the rainbow seemed to bridge the way to another, brighter world. As the Walhall march died in Paul's ears he found himself in the open air, and he thought it all over as he slowly went with the crowd down the hill, that new Mount of Olives trod by the feet of musical martyrs. He had a programme, but he was too confused, too overcome by the clangor of his brain-particles, to read it. He was not dreaming, nor yet was he awake; he was Wagnerized. The first attack is not always fatal, but it is always severe, even to the point of pain. Paul Godard had become a Wagnerite, and his Nietzsche and Schopenhauer skins melted from him as melts the snow in sunshine.

Striking through his many exalted moods was the consciousness of having recognized one of the Rhine Daughters. It was the contralto, an Eastern girl from Maine. Rue Towne was her odd name, and she had been once a pupil of a New England vocal school, but she had lived that down, and after the usual hard, interesting struggle abroad she had reached Baireuth.

VENUS OR VALKYR?

Paul remembered her well. A blonde girl, eyes indescribably gray, with dark lashes, a face full of interesting accents, a rhythmic chin and cheekbones that told of resolution. Her figure was lovely, and Paul resolved to call on her the very next day.

He soon discovered Rue's address; Baireuth is small and full of information for the curious. Paul on Monday morning went to the Alexanderstrasse, where she resided, only to find her at a rehearsal of Die Walküre. He was rather put out, as he was accustomed to accomplish what he wanted without much exertion. He then bethought him of Helena, the Roumanian beauty, and he warmed at the recollection of a glance he had received the afternoon previous. That, and the hand pressure, had been unmistakable. So he went to the Sonne Hotel and sent up his card. The three ladies were at breakfast. Would Mr. Godard call in an hour?

Paul cursed his luck and walked to Wahnfried, wondering if he was to be bored during his stay. The reaction from the exalted condition after Rhinegold had set in. Paul was not a beer-drinker, so he could not avail himself of the consolations offered by Gambrinus, the Drowsy Deity of Germany. He had taken a pint of bad champagne and some tough chicken and slept badly. His cigar, too, was abominable, and he felt absolutely disillusioned as he paced the historic garden of Wahnfried. The true Wagnerite is always in heaven or hades.

There is no middle-distance in his picture of life and art. At Wagner's grave Paul felt a return of the thrill, but it passed away at the barking of a boarhound. He went slowly toward the hotel and was in such a perverse mood that he avoided it and turned into the Ludwigstrasse. Then he met some one.

A girl passed him, gave him a shy, half-startled glance, hesitated, and spoke to him. It was Rue Towne.

"Mr. Godard, I found your card a moment ago. I am very glad to see you. How did you like Rhinegold?"

Paul was standing in the street, the girl looking down into his eyes; he made a conventional answer, their hands touched, and they went down the street together.

That afternoon Paul received a pretty note from the Roumanian. She wrote of her sorrow at his not having called again, and asked him to join them during the first entr'acte of Die Walküre. He tossed the note away, for his brain was filled with the vision of a girl in a straight-brimmed straw hat, a girl with a voice like a wooing clarinet and eyes that were dewy with desire. Paul was hard hit, and, as one nail drives out another, the blonde woman supplanted the brunette in his easily stirred imagination.

The first act of Die Walküre did not lay the fair ghost in his brain; he went out on the esplanade and encountered the three Roumanians. Helena detached herself and came to him with that

VENUS OR VALKYR?

gracious gait and proud lift of head and throat that gave her a touch of royalty. She reproached him with her magnetic gaze, and soon the pair were strolling in the leafy lanes about the theatre.

Paul had never met a woman who mentally tantalized him as did Helena. She had a manner of half uttering a sentence, of putting a nuance into her question that interested while it irritated him. Artistic people are mutually attracted, and there was a savor in the personality of this distinguished girl that was infinitely enticing to his cultivated taste and at the same time slightly enigmatic. Without effort they glided into confidences, and the Sword-motive sounding for the second act found them old friends. Youth is not the time for halting compromise.

Lilli Lehmann's art took Paul out of himself, and the beauty and vigor of the act stirred him again. But he could not recapture the first fine, careless rapture of the night before. To the nerves, virginal of Wagner, that thrill comes once only.

In the long intermission Paul found Helena and took her to the crowded café across the road to get something to eat and drink. It was a quarter after seven, and Wagner wears on the stomach. Even a poetical Roumanian girl has earthly appetites. So they drank champagne and ate pasties of goose liver, and confessions were many. Nothing establishes a strong bond

BEDOUINS

of sympathy like the hunger and thirst of two healthy young humans. Paul seemed to have forgotten Rue and the splendour of her hair and complexion. He was rapidly losing his head in the subtle blandishments of the Eastern woman. He saw that she was a coquette, but her seriousness, her fierceness, that broke through the shell of silky manners, gave him a glimpse of a woman worth winning, and he was just gambler enough, American enough to dare. When he left her he carried away a look that was an unequivocal challenge.

Paul's brain was on fire during the Ride of the Valkyries, and hardly realized that it was Hans Richter's masterly reading. The stage failed to interest him until he discovered Rue in Valkyrean garb, and then he watched with his soul in his eyes. Her profile, so charming in its irregularity; her freedom of pose, her heroic action filled him with admiration. By the light from the stage he read her name, Fräulein Rue Towne, and she was the last in the list of the Valkyries. He watched with indifferent gaze the close of the act, and mentally voted the Paris version of the Magic-Fire scene far superior to Baireuth's.

He went toward the Hotel Sonne, as he had promised to sup with Helena, and wondered how he could see Rue that night. The American girl seemed something infinitely sweet, healthy, sunswept in nature compared with her Slavic rival.

"By Jove," said Paul aloud, "it's a case of

rouge et noir, and I'm in for it and no mistake."
Paul was fond of polyphony.

IV

After supper he suggested to Helena the Sammet Garden. The artists always flocked there and it might prove interesting. Although a chaperon was a necessity, Helena persuaded the princess that she could go out just once in the American fashion. It would be so novel. Paul pleaded and, of course, won. The young people hardly spoke as they went down the dark street to the garden. The air was full of electricity. A touch, a glance, and a storm would be precipitated. So they reached the garden and found a seat near enough the house to be tortured by Herr Sammet's crazy trombone. At the same table was a black-bearded little man dressed in white flannels.

"It is the Sâr Peladan; I know him by his musk," said Helena discontentedly, and they changed their seats.

"What a decadent you are!" said Godard laughingly.

"Yes. I believe sometimes I can think with my nose, my smelling sense is so keen. I can almost divine approaching enemies. Who is that girl staring at you so hard, M. Godard, a very pretty blonde; she looks like an American? No, not near the house — there, over there!" Helena reminded Paul of a cat that lifts a threatening furry back when she scents a hostile dog.

"Oh, Lord!" he groaned. "It must be Rue. That settles me for good." It was Rue, and she had never looked lovelier. The slight bruise under her eyes betokened emotional exhaustion. She was dressed in white, and the simplicity of her gown and its charming fit made the German women plainer. Paul's heart knocked against his ribs as he returned her constrained bow. He saw that she had quietly and earnestly examined Helena, and as the eyes of the women met antagonism kindled. But the American girl was mistress of herself. She began to talk to the group of artists about her, while Helena sulked and glowered at Paul's too openly expressed admiration.

"You admire your own countrywomen, do you not, M. Godard?" she asked, and the inflection in her voice was cruelly sarcastic. Before Paul could answer she touched his arm softly and said:

"If you can't look at me when I talk to you, why, you may take me home."

Paul at once begged her pardon, called for his reckoning and they prepared to leave the garden. He did not again salute Rue Towne, for she was talking earnestly to an ugly old fat man with a grey beard and a Wagnerian forehead half a foot high. But from the tail of his eye he saw that she was fully conscious of his departure. Scarlet spots came into her face, and

VENUS OR VALKYR?

as Paul walked down the garden steps he felt as if two eyes burned into his back. Then he did what other desperate men have done under similar circumstances. He made violent love to Helena, and it relieved the pain of his heart. But the girl was capricious, and only by dint of magnificent lying did he finally force her hand into his. They were now walking toward the Hofgarten, down a deserted street. The many bells of Baireuth told them that it was a quarter past eleven, and the moon rode tenderly in the blue. It was a night made for soft vows and kisses, and as Paul walked he thought of Rue; Helena fell to dreaming of the prince in her native Roumania who had played the weakling to her strong woman's heart, and thus the pair reached the hotel, and after a brief parley at its door said good night and parted.

O blessed love, that can at least console two hearts glowing for the absent!

Paul awoke next morning with what the hardheaded Germans call a moral headache. He had a bad taste in his conscience, and he decided to call as soon as possible on Rue. It was nearly eleven before he got to her house. As she had no rehearsal for Siegfried, she received him. He thought that she was distant, but he talked fast and earnestly, and soon the ice began to thaw. Paul felt happy. Helena appealed to his decadent taste, but Rue was as the perfume of the morning. He told her so, and explained at great length and with considerable ingenuity how he came in the company of a lone young woman. Her two chaperons — Paul fancied two sounded more imposing — had gone by mistake to the garden of the Sonne Hotel; that is why he left so soon with the lady, who was only a recent acquaintance.

He felt Rue's eyes on him as he wove this roundelay, and, feeling hot about the neck and a little fearful of his ability to keep up the strain much longer, he suddenly grasped the girl, crying out, and most sincerely:

"O Rue! why do we waste time talking about a woman I never cared for and never expect to see again. I love you, I love you, my darling! Kiss me just once and tell me you care a little for me."

As he fell upon her she was taken off her guard, and the inevitable happened. She kissed Paul and he placed a big ring on her finger, and left the house an hour later an engaged and also a much be-perjured man. He was happy until he thought of Helena.

That evening when Siegfried was finished Paul walked arm and arm with Rue down the hill to Sammet's. As they entered they brushed against three ladies, and Paul said aloud: "Oh, Lord!"

The next day Rue had to go to a rehearsal for the Rhine Daughters in Die Götterdämmerung, and Paul was whistling the Spring Song from Die Walküre in his room when a knock at his door brought the news that a lady wished to see him. He wondered who the lady was, and, as the parlor of the house had been turned into a bedroom, he put on his hat and went into the hall, to be confronted by Helena, shamefaced but resolute.

"Come out into the street," he begged, for in her implacable eyes he read signs of the approaching storm.

They silently descended to a lower étage. Then she turned and faced him:

"So you didn't come to me this morning," she said. Roumania excited was a stirring spectacle, nevertheless Paul wished that he was up the Hudson playing golf.

He endeavored to placate her. Helena, angered at her loss of dignity in condescending to call on this man, reproached him bitterly, and it seemed to him that she was about to sing the picturesque songs of hate which Carmen Sylva has made known to us, when they reached the street. Then her rage vanished in a moment.

"You conceited man, and you really took me in solemn earnest! I fancied the Americans had a sense of humor. Pooh! You're not a man to love more than a moment, anyhow," and she went on her way laughing mockingly, leaving Paul shamefaced, angered, his self-love all bruised and his senses aroused, for Helena wrathful was more beautiful than Helena amiable.

He was so distressed in mind that he only sat through one act of Die Götterdämmerung; his

Wagner madness seemed to have evaporated. He hovered around the back of the theatre, and caught a glimpse of Rue getting in a carriage with the same fat old German — her singing-teacher, he fancied.

Although it was late, he called at her house. She had not yet arrived, the maid told him. He mooned about disconsolately until one o'clock, keeping at a safe distance from the Hotel Sonne. Then he wearily went to bed and dreamed that the Nornes were chasing him down Fifth Avenue.

The next morning he called again on Rue. She sent down word that she was tired. He called again in the afternoon; she was not at home. In the evening, feeling as if he were going mad, he was told that she had gone out and would not be back until late. He hung around the house in a hungry-dog fashion, smiling bitterly at times and beginning to doubt even his own intentions. But no Rue.

He went home at last, and in a rage of love and jealousy he sat down and wrote to Rue this letter:

"Rue, my Rue, darling, what is the matter? Have I offended you? Why did you not see me to-day, to-night? Oh, how lonely was the street, how sad my heart! I thought of Verlaine's 'It rains in my heart as it rains in the town.' Why don't you see me? You are mine; you swore it. My sweet girl, whose heart is as fragrant as new-mown hay! Darling, you must

VENUS OR VALKYR?

see me to-morrow — to-day — for I am writing to you in the early, early morning. You know that you promised to come to me next year in America. Only think, sweetheart, what joy then! The sky is aflame with love. We walk slowly under few soft spring stars, and your hand is in mine, and that night, that night your heart will sob on my breast, my lovely woman, and your heart will fiercely beat as we both slip over the hills to heaven. Rue, you will make me a poet. Only tell me, I beg of you, the hour when I may see you."

Then Paul threw himself on the bed, but not to sleep. It was daybreak, and the Teutonic chanticleer of the dawn had lusty lungs, and it was almost time for coffee. He dressed in feverish haste, went out of doors, secured a messenger and despatched the letter. He walked up and down the Lisztstrasse for twenty minutes, and his emotion was so great at the sight of the boy returning, a letter in hand, that he retreated into the doorway and awaited the news. It was brief. He read this in Rue's firm handwriting:

"Your friend Helena has told me all. Here is your ring."

There was no signature.

Then Paul did what most cowards do. He went to the other woman. The storm in his soul might be allayed, and he could have the pleasure of showing Rue that she was not necessary to him. Of course the jealousy of Helena had spoiled his game; for he really had meant to be sincere with Rue, so he told himself in the inward, eloquent manner which paves hell with composite intentions. It was all clear to him. Helena loved him, else why did she tell Rue of his double-dealing? It gave him a glowing feeling again in his distracted bosom, and as he walked into the Hotel Sonne he said between clutched teeth:

"Black wins!"

He was met by a polite portier, who told him that his friends had left on the early train for Vienna. But there was a letter!

Heart-sick and with trembling hands he tore open the envelope.

"Did you really think I loved an American when I can have a Roumanian? Better console your singer."

No signature.

"When does the next train leave for Paris?" asked Paul of the polite portier.

. . . .

There is a rumor in society that Paul Godard is engaged to Edith Vicker. He never goes to a Wagner music-drama, and is passionately addicted to cabaret dancing.

Americans are versatile.

V
THE CARDINAL'S FIDDLE

YAKOV leaned out of his window and greedily listened to the Cardinal playing his fiddle. The window was small and under a hot roof. From it a view of the great palace of his Eminence was easy, for the house of Yakov's mother stood in a narrow court at the rear, and was a low-sized building, not far from the Cathedral which dominated this old-fashioned and once aristocratic section of the city. The bedroom of the boy was on a level with the living-room of the Cardinal — a tall, spare old man with mild eyes and ascetic face. His bushy white hair and ruddy complexion, coupled with a high, hawk-like nose, gave him the appearance, in Yakov's eyes, of a benevolent bird of exotic origin. Stranger still was his passion for music. At least once a day he could be seen by the lad, walking with long, elastic strides about the large bare room, a violin tucked under his chin, his eyes closed, and he fiddling as if rehearsing for a classical concert. Yakov knew it was "classical" music because he couldn't make head or tail of it, although he was studying the instrument himself at the big conservatory on the square. But he was only a beginner — that's what his cross teacher told him when his lesson was a poor one — and he realized the fact, while the Cardinal — oh! he played everything difficult, and always without notes.

He wondered why this kindly old gentleman in the queer dress should fiddle in the great palace across the way; he, so rich and powerful, doing for fun what the poor little Yiddish boy did as a task. When Yakov could play he wouldn't live in a palace, but would try to get a job in a theatre orchestra. His mother answered his query, "What is a cardinal?" with a vague, "Oh, he is a sort of high rabbi," which didn't tell her son much. He was brought up in the orthodox faith, went to Shool — the synagogue — and was careful to eat no food that had not been prepared in Kosher fashion. This last practice brought him into conflict with the boys of his class at the public school around the corner. They were American born, though many of foreign descent. That made no difference, for, as much as they quarrelled with one another, they were a unit as to the undesirability of the Jew. Their teacher had scolded, had even punished them, but uselessly. They were sarcastic, were these boys of Italian, Irish and German parents, calling aloud, "Micky," "Dutchy," "Guinney," "Wop," but for Yakov and his like—in the majority at the school—they had choicer terms: "Sheeny" "Kike!" "Mekmek!" Yakov didn't much mind the nicknames.

THE CARDINAL'S FIDDLE

He only feared the suddenly delivered punches at his back, the vise-like grip of "Jimmy the Brick" (self-christened) on his neck, and the hateful grin with which a ham sandwich would be thrust into his mouth. This last was the supreme insult. If he did not complain to his teacher, it was because he feared reprisals. So he only told his mother, with tears in his large, dark, expressive eyes, and she comforted him. She said it was the glory of his race, this badge of suffering, these insults from the Gentiles. He must not fight back, but meekly endure. Jehovah would watch over him. She was a decent widow woman, who had a small dressmaking business in her house and barely supported herself and child, also giving him a musical education. Oh! to see him a great violinist! She loved music, and as she worked her sewing-machine she hummed to its rhythms. Once, many years ago, she had heard in Lemberg, her Galician birthplace, the greatest violinist in the world, Joseph Joachim, and one of her race. She was unmarried then, yet she made a silent vow that if ever she had a son . . .

She had Yakov now, and his father was gone. She always said to him — dead. But she knew better. He had deserted her for another woman, left her without a dollar, and she had been fighting for ten years to keep their heads above water. Living in this humble yet genteel court behind the Cathedral, she dreamed of Yakov's future, and she cried with joy when the teacher at the conservatory grudgingly admitted that the boy had talent and might — he coughed his reservations — with hard work make a fair musician. Yakov went to school and in the afternoons practised. The weather was warm, windows were opened, and he attentively heard the fiddle of the Cardinal.

The music was a succession of beautiful sounds for the young visionary. His eyes glittering, his lips apart, his arms tightly folded about his thin little frame, he listened as if to the voice of God. The Cardinal played the slow movement of Mendelssohn's concerto, and, threadbare as has become this familiar song, to Yakov it was an enchantment. Its obvious sentiment seemed a call from his dead father in heaven. When the music ceased he involuntarily stretched aloft his arms. The eye of the Cardinal must have caught the glint of white — the boy was in his shirt-sleeves — and came to the window cautiously, peering across to Yakov. He vaguely smiled, and to Yakov's sorrow he closed the window, yet the sound of his fiddle softly echoed in the ears of the boy.

Every evening he stationed himself at the same spot, but the Cardinal did not play. Yakov yearned for his music. His own cheap red fiddle became hateful to him. Its rasping tones when he attempted scales extinguished his ambition. One day his mother said in her purring Yiddish: "Yakov, you must be more industrious, else the gentleman at the conservatory

THE CARDINAL'S FIDDLE

will send you home." Even that didn't arouse him. He suddenly took to playing in the court with the other boys after school. Such rough games! He stood a lot of kicking and punching, especially from Jimmy the Brick, who, after all, wasn't a bad-hearted chap. He once grabbed Yakov's lunch-box and critically swallowed the contents, which pleased him, as he liked full-flavored food. "Say, Kike, that's not bad grub. I like your stuffed fish better than the macaroni of that Wop kid Tony." With this backing of the boss Yakov enjoyed comparative peace. He had thought of revenge, of organizing into a compact phalanx the large body of Jewish boys at the school, but his mother's advice and the patience of his race dissuaded him from active rebellion. He let things slide along, and in the meantime his music was almost neglected. In vain did his teacher rap his knuckles with the fiddle-bow and threaten him with dismissal. Yakov knew the crosspatch wouldn't keep his word, for he was a pay pupil; not much pay, to be sure; anyhow, not a charity scholar.

The magic of a windless June night transformed the old Red Lion court into an operatic picture. Moonlit, it recalled a prosperous past that had hardly modulated into its present middle-class shabbiness. Old houses, colonial in style, but sadly defaced by time, slept tranquilly in the magnetic rays of a moon which breasted the low housetops. The din and gabble had ceased, the only noise being the sound of hammered iron on the anvil of the blacksmith's at the corner. So changed were times that the legend over the door of the smithy read, "Sokolov & Grünstein — Horseshoers." The ancient and honorable profession had been wrested from sturdy English and Irish hands by the more persistent hosts from southeastern Europe. For Yakov the change meant nothing, but it gave extreme pain to Jimmy's parents, and so Jimmy, with his faithful band, was in the habit of yelling defiant and insulting words at the two blacksmiths, though keeping at a safe distance. The rhythmic tapping of the hammers brought peace to Yakov, who stood in his window regarding with awakened curiosity the spectacle of the Cardinal's living-room, lighted for the first time in weeks; perhaps — ! Presently the sound of a fiddle oozed through the open space. He was back, the Cardinal with his fiddle. What was he playing? Hymn tunes, surely. First, the Adeste Fideles, which Yakov remembered because in a moment of condescending generosity Jimmy had taken him to Vespers at the Cathedral and had told him the name of the music he had heard.

Then the tune shifted to a more solemn, a celestial tune, indeed, which the listener couldn't place. He didn't know it was the O Jesu, by Haydn, but that didn't matter; his ear was ravished by its pleading strains, and he hung out of his perch, tremulously absorbing every tone. The Cardinal's humor shifted. He dashed off a

THE CARDINAL'S FIDDLE

gay Tipperary jig, and followed this with The Valley Lay Smiling Before Me, and The Harp of Tara. Yakov felt that the violinist must be an Irishman, but ever so different from the noisy Jimmy. Yet Irish!

What, what! He pinched himself as the grave music of the Kol Nidré, the sacred tune sounded on the Day of Atonement, came swelling across the Cardinal's windows. The Kol Nidré, that immemorial cantillation of the Hebrews, in it compressed the dolors of the ages, and perhaps first chanted in the house of Egyptian bondage, perhaps out of the dim centuries before Egypt, before the shadowy Sumerians! Who knows? What concerned the boy was the strange happening — a potentate of the Gentile Church playing on a fiddle the grand and venerable hymn of the Jews. But that he was fascinated by the music he would have rushed down to his mother to tell her the glad tidings. She knew of the playing across in the palace, and was pleased because of Yakov's evident interest. She would welcome the return of the Cardinal, for her boy would be again spurred to study. He couldn't leave the window till the last note had been squeezed from the august and mournful melody.

In a fever Yakov seized his tiny instrument and lovingly mimicked the Cardinal. Its squeak reached the priest, who came to the window and waited until Yakov's imperfect interpretation of the Kol Nidré ended, and, smiling a kind smile that melted the heart within the bosom of the boy, he waved a slender hand, as if to say, "I salute a brother artist!" It was too much for Yakov, who ran to his mother's sewing-room, there to pour out his joy and receive her gentle blessing. He, too, would play the fiddle like the Cardinal—play the Kol Nidré for a hall full of listeners, who would applaud him! The mighty Cardinal had played the Kol Nidré for the poor little Jew boy, and he hadn't even bowed his profound gratitude!

On wings of song, he mounted the stairway to his garret, but the music was no longer heard, though the windows were still alight. Not able to control himself, Yakov took his instrument, and, all the while playing, marched down-stairs into the court, and in the mystic moonshine he played on, played the Kol Nidré. Soon the gang surrounded him, and Jimmy the Brick cried: "Aw, give us a rest with that tune. Play a coon song." Yakov only shook his head and kept on playing.

"Stop it, I say!" yelled Jimmy. "We want none of yer Kike music in this court. D'ye hear?" Yakov still played, and the tune rang out with the terror and desolation of the Day of Atonement.

"Hit him, Tony! Grab his fiddle, you Wop!" hoarsely commanded the leader. The boys closed about him and in a twinkling the current of the music was cut off, the red violin smashed into a hundred bits, the bow snapped in two and

THE CARDINAL'S FIDDLE

its coarse hair twisted about Yakov's neck. He fought silently, tearlessly. The firm of Sokolov & Grünstein came to his rescue, and, being muscular men, they routed the band and sent the victim to his home with consoling phrases. But he was hopeless. That another fiddle might be bought for him found no place in his whirling imagination. He had been cruelly treated. Why should he be so punished? As he sank on his knees at his attic window tears flowed and sobs followed. Yakov mourned and would not be comforted. And across the court in the chamber of the palace the Cardinal played with exquisite melancholy that antique Hebraic tune, the Kol Nidré.

VI

RENUNCIATION

The hearts of some women are as a vast cathedral. There are its gorgeous high altars, its sounding gloom, its lofty arches, and perhaps in an obscure niche burns a tiny taper before the votive shrine. And many pass through life with this taper unlighted, despite the pomp and ceremonial of the conjugal comedy. Others carry in the little chapel of their hearts a solitary glimmering lamp of love that only flames out with death.

A GRAND piano, its burnished ivory teeth gleaming in the candle-light, stood near the open window, and at it one lounged and idly preluded Schumann-like harmonies that questioned the night. Outside a veiled fumidity, behind which lurked thunderous prospects; the air was still with languorous anticipation, and the month of the year was April. He would not have been human and an artist to have withstood the dumb depression of the moment. Snatches of heavily brocaded harmonies of Chopin, mute interrogations of Brahms, and furtive glitterings of Liszt vibrated through the chamber. One sultry chord, persistently repeated and unresolved, told the temper of him who played.

It was a sober apartment; a half-score of wax tapers sang with a bunch of tuberoses a sweet duo.

RENUNCIATION

A few chairs, some music scattered about, a tall bookcase, gaunt and shadowy in the background, and a polished floor made the ensemble of an artist's living-room. The playing grew vaguer and the night without more menacing. Then the first eight or ten bars of the prelude to Tristan und Isolde forced into shape on the keyboard and — hush! a delicate knock at the door. He harshly called, "Entrez!" She was without a wrap, her head enveloped in a filmy burnoose. She faltered, then moved to him as moves a sleep-walker. "I know that it is wrong, but I — how can I help it? I have come to you — and you?" She paused, her face illuminated by love-doubt. His voice was muffled when he answered her, "Pray be seated, madame."

She divined his reluctance: "We leave tomorrow, and you must play for me once more."

"I could have called at your hotel," he gently replied.

Impetuously she cried: "I have risked much to be near you, to hear you play; yet you stand coldly, and after yesterday — Ah, you forget!"

"I do not forget," he replied.

She moved toward him; his reserve vanished and he advanced with both hands outstretched. "Dearest, it is madness. See, it is late; you will be missed, and the night bodes a storm. Play! I would play for you if Paradise threatened and hell yawned rather than refuse you."

"Play!" she cried. "Play for me Chopin, but do not come near me." He shivered, and their eyes kissed, hers burning like misty-green signals of love and sorrow; then he faced the night for a moment, and turning to the piano began without preluding.

It was the Second Impromptu of Chopin, the rarely heard one in the key of F sharp, major mode. As he struck the octave in the bass the approaching storm muttered in the west, the wind soughed into the room, and the flame of the wax tapers flickered faint messages to the tuberoses. She on the couch sighed softly. The magic of Chopin enveloped them as the plaintive theme broke the air into melodic ripples. It sang her into depths of dreams, anterior to which lurked other dreams — dreams with soft-sounding syllables, dreams that lapped her consciousness into the golden gloom of drugged slumber, dreams opal-tinted and music-melancholy beyond compare. She swooned and then swam out to the infinite with bold, blissful strokes, for he was playing with rare cunning the closing choral-like measures of the first part of the Impromptu.

The moan without deepened into a roar, then came a vermilion flash followed by a crash of thunder. The lights were extinguished, all but one, swayed feebly in the rush of the wind, and the tuberoses listened thirstily to the plash of the new-born rain.

He had begun the D major section of the Im-

RENUNCIATION

promptu; the rhythmical swing of the bass seemed a proud spirit defying destiny, and the massive chords, with virile assertive tones, blended with the night and roared answer to the thunder's bellow. They rose to a crescendo, they dominated all, for the man within was storming out his resolves and passions on the keyboard. The fury increased to a sheer height of tone; then, melting away into a mere echo, it almost fainted. His soul chased hers and together they followed the enigmatic tones of that modulation which is an abysm betwixt fragrant meads, and warns them that seek its depths. The lovely F major part glimmered in the air.

> "Come back to me, to the first of all;
>   Let us learn and love it over again.
> Let us now forget and now recall,
>   Break the rosary in a pearly rain,
> And gather what we let fall."

"Browning," she softly mused, "and life." The plot thickened, the harmony grew denser — a musical palimpsest lay before them, and as they strove to unweave its meaning they shuddered at the gulf. Weary and panting in spirit they stared askance and questioned the future. "Not that," the music implored. Then burst that delicious cascade of silvery scales. They coruscated, they foamed, they boiled with melodic laughter. It seemed as if God was with the world and he and she heard the lark trilling to the dawn as hand in hand they mounted in their dizzy flight. Their naked, unabashed souls groped in the azure and they carolled that song which is as old as eternity. They fell through space into fathomless twilight, and the piano sang the echo-like refrain of the first motif. It was the swan-song of their hopes. The heavy-scented night spoke softly to their hearts; a nightingale dimly piped in the distance, and with velvety clangor the music ceased.

He remained at the piano. She rose. Without were odors and starlight. The two drank each other's gaze with the thirst of lost souls. Then she went into the night, and the other one, staring at the tuberoses, heard their perfumed murmur: "Renounce thou shalt; thou shalt renounce."

VII
THE VISION MALEFIC

"To be in Heaven the second, he disdains:
So now the first in Hell and flames he reigns,
Crown'd once with joy and light: crown'd now with fire
    and pains."
—*Phineas Fletcher* (1582).

I AM not a diabolist. I was an agnostic until
. . . I have read Huysmans and I do not believe
he ever saw half he describes. Yet I, and in
commonplace America, have seen things, have
heard things, that would make mad the group
of Parisian occultists. I dislike publicity, but
Vance Thompson has asked me to relate the
story, and so I mean to give it, names and all,
with the faint hope that it may serve as a warning to callow astrologists, and all the younger
generation affected by the writings of impious
men who deny the existence of the devil.

More than twenty years ago I was the organist
of a Roman Catholic church in the lower part
of my city. I had studied the instrument in
Germany and believed in Johann Sebastian
Bach. I played and pedalled fugues on weekdays for my own pleasure, and on Sundays executed with unction easy masses by Bordoni,
Mercadante, and Haydn; my choir was not an
ambitious one. The stipendium was small, the

work light, and the two priests amiable enough. One, a German, Father Oelschlager, was the rector. His assistant was an Irishman with French blood in his veins. His name — shall I ever forget his name and face? — was Father Michael Moreau. He was crazy about music and occultism. The former he made no secret of; the latter I discovered only after a long acquaintance. Moreau came to the organ-loft when I practised on week-days, sang a little, and feasted much on Bach chorales. Urged often to visit his room, I did so, and he showed me rare black-letter missals, and later the backs of a number of old books whose titles I could not decipher. I am no Latinist, yet I knew these volumes were written neither in Latin nor Greek. The characters I had never seen before, and when I remarked their strangeness, Father Moreau smiled and even laughed as I quoted Poe: "the volumes of the Magi — in the iron-bound melancholy volumes of the Magi."

Music led us to discuss religion, and my friend astonished me by his erudition. His sensitive features would become illuminated when he spoke of the strange tales of the Talmud. "Oh, my God!" he would cry with a patibulary gesture. "Why hast Thou not vouchsafed us more light?" And then would beg for Bach, and on the mighty stream of the D minor fugue his harassed mind seemed to float and find comfort. As time wore on he grew morbid, morose, reticent, and devoted himself to his dull duties with a

THE VISION MALEFIC

fanaticism that was almost harsh. The parishioners noticed it, and his reputation for saintliness increased. His confessional was always crowded and his sermons remarkable for the acerbity, the awful pictures he made of the sufferings of the damned and of the relentlessness of God's wrath. His superior, good-natured Father Oelschlager, bade the other look at the cheerful side of the question, to believe more in God's mellowness and sweetness, and would quote Cardinal Newman's Lead Kindly Light, and certain comforting texts from the Scriptures, and then smoke his pipe. But the ascetic temperament of Moreau barred all attempts at palliation or attenuation of the God of Hosts, of the God who laid low the pride of Greece and Rome. Life to him was a cancer to be extirpated, and he confessed to me one night after rehearsal that he had almost doubted God's existence and courted suicide after reading Renan's Vie de Jésus. I suggested change of scene, less strenuous labors, above all, the world, music, and athletics. My advice availed not, and I saw that Father Moreau was fast becoming a monomaniac. His sermons during the hot summer were devoted to the personality of the devil, to his corporeal existence, to his daily presence in the marts of mankind; and so constant was his harping on this theme that Father Oelschlager had to forbid him the subject. "It is so warm, my son! Why, then, do you hold forth on hell? Let the poor people hear more of the crystal rivers, the green meads of the New Jerusalem. It would be more seasonable." Moreau frowned, but obeyed his superior.

With the autumn and winter his habits became more secretive, his visits to me less frequent, and his air of detachment most melancholy. Advent saw him a mere wraith of a man, worn by speculation, devoured by an interior flame, a flame that was wasting his very soul to despair. He seldom conversed with me, although I watched him anxiously and occasionally interrogated him regarding his health. At last I spoke to his associate, but encountered an easy-going philosophic spirit, which assured me Father Moreau was going through what most young priests should. He was at the period of unfaith, was nettled by doubt, and after he had wrestled with Satan, and won the good fight, he would again become normal. This seemed consoling though vague.

The day before Christmas I promised that I would not send a substitute to play the midnight mass at the church. Our church was the only one in the city where the old-fashioned mass at twelve o'clock on Christmas Eve was celebrated. It is located near the river, and my journey was a long one, for I lived up-town. I ate a six o'clock supper and went to bed, telling them to arouse me at a quarter before eleven. I wished to be fresh for the early service. By eleven I was out on the street, and took a car bound south. I reached the church in time,

THE VISION MALEFIC

and soon the solemn high mass began. My choir had with elaborate care prepared Cherubini's mass, and despite the poor organ, the extra chorus and much enthusiasm made some effect. The congregation was attentive, and Father Oelschlager delivered a short, happy sermon, urging his flock to rejoice at the birth of the Babe of Bethlehem, Jesus the Infant Christ, uncrucified, but newly born into a world of toil and sin for our redemption. At the consecration of the host the good rector's beaming faith was most edifying. He was served by Father Moreau, a melancholy deacon, indeed. "Ite Missa Est" pronounced, the faithful dismissed, I was overjoyed at the release, for I was tired. The choir chatted about the service, the singing, and at last I was alone. I placed the musicbooks back in the tall Gothic cupboard, closed the manuals of my instrument, and put on my overcoat. It must have been half past one, perhaps quarter of two, and I relished the prospect of my arrival home, where a warm breakfast would be awaiting me, and then once more to bed, for I had to play the regular half past ten o'clock Christmas mass for the benefit of the sleepy ones, who loved their couch better than their Christ.

Father Moreau met me at the bottom of the choir-loft steps. He was dressed for the street, his eyes were blazing, and as he took my arm his fingers were vise-like. "Will you come with me?" he asked. I was startled. I explained

BEDOUINS

that I would not have much rest, nor should he waste his sleeping time on the dismal, cold streets; besides, I was hungry. I feared that he was about to deluge me with more of his studies in the customs of the early Gnostics, and, to be quite frank, I was worn out and not in a receptive humor for such untoward cryptic wisdom. Any other time — "Will you come with me?" he reiterated, and the clutch on my arm became oppressive. "Where?" I asked, for I hated to affront a friend. "Will you come with me?"

By this time the church was quite empty, and I pushed out into the street. It was dark and snowing hard. We walked toward the street, and as we neared the corner I heard the lucky sound of a horse-car — there were no trolleys then. I excused myself, ran and caught the car; the priest, following, sat down beside me. I paid both fares, and as I had nothing to say we preserved a sad silence. The mean light, the deserted streets, the lonely car, and the muffled strokes of the horses' hoofs on the snow chilled my soul. I looked sideways at Father Moreau. He was reading a big parchment-covered book, which I saw by the dim lamplight was entitled Le Satanisme, by Jules Bois. I was shocked. A priest fresh from the holy sacrifice of the mass devouring the blasphemies that I was sure were in the gruesome volume, alarmed my piety. Presently he saw me and shut its leaves. "There are curious things in it, my dear friend," he muttered, and his voice came from across a waste of sorrow. "Curious things; but you are a believer, are you not?" he eagerly repeated. "I am," I replied devoutly, and I crossed myself. He fairly jumped at me, his eyes wide open and full of devouring flames. "Will you come with me?" he almost screamed, and for the fourth time. "East Street," called out the conductor, and rather than let my half-mad companion alone — he surely must have been mad — I left the car with him, the conductor gazing after us with cynical eyes. He evidently took us for belated revellers.

We walked slowly for ten minutes until we arrived in front of a sad-looking church, and then I stopped: "The place is not open yet; they do not have Christmas service until five o'clock." For the last time my companion whispered, "Will you come with me?" and, pushing past me, struck three times on the big doors. A small postern gate opened at once and we entered the vaulted passageway. I trembled at the strangeness of the adventure, and held fast to Moreau, for it was pitch black, and while I heard soft footfalls beside me — the footfalls of an unknown man — I could not see my hand before my face. We must have traversed a long yard, for the wind blew freely about me; I heard it playing on the housetops like a balloon in distress. Yet it felt as if issuing from a sepulchre, and my heart went to my empty stomach. Even in my growing terror I craved for coffee; its aroma would have made me stronger for this inhuman cruise. We went down eleven steps — I counted them — my conductors on either side of me. Dampness and malodors warned me of our proximity to some ancient cellarage, some forgotten catacombs, wherein Father Moreau expected to give me a sacerdotal surprise, a revival perhaps of an antique and early Christian ritual. I feebly applauded his intentions, but wished he had chosen some other time and that the surroundings had been less sinister.

At last we paused and descended another flight of steps — this time I didn't number them, for the cold was intense, and it was with relief that we suddenly arrived in a dimly lighted and warm chapel. It was empty, devoid of pews, of chairs, of furnishings of any sort, except, at the upper end, a small votive altar. Before it swung a lamp of Byzantine workmanship, in which burned a solitary tongue of yellow flame. The lamp swayed rhythmically, and on the altar were two tall tapers, lighted and perfumed. And then my eyes rested on the spot where should have been the tabernacle, surmounted by the gold cross. Judge of my consternation when I saw, saw as distinctly as I see the pen which traces these letters, a huge bronze serpent, with overlapping, glistening, metallic scales. The eyes of this python were almost feminine, and their regard gentle, reproachful, and voluptuous. My knees bent beneath me and my face was wet with fright.

THE VISION MALEFIC

"You are a believer, then?" crooned a dull voice in my ear. It was Moreau. He had thrown off his outer wrap and stood in a black soutane. He was white with emotion and said in tenderest accents: "Listen; be my friend. Do not desert me at the crisis of my life. It is to be my first mass, my first three o'clock mass. My deacon is already at the altar. Be the solitary worshipper. It will be a low mass — remember, a low mass!" He spoke clearly, rapidly, sanely, and seeing that I had something more than a lunatic to deal with, I removed my overcoat and knelt down near the altar just as Father Moreau ascended its steps, his assistant holding the end of his *black* canonicals. If it had not been for the apparition of the serpent, I might have fancied that I was assisting at the lonely, pious vigil of a parochial curate. But the eyes of the serpent devoured mine, and I had none for the two silhouetted figures that went through with febrile velocity the familiar motions of the mass. It was low mass, and from the introit to the preface the space was scarcely appreciable. I heard mumblings, and the air became chillier as the celebrants moved and bowed or extended arms; the air grew colder, denser, and tenser. It vibrated like the wires of a monstrous zither, and my temples throbbed as if in the midst of a magnetic storm. I felt that I was nearing a great catastrophe, that God had abandoned His universe to its wicked will, and that I must sob, or scream, or pray, or die, or be damned forever, or — the tap of the silvery little bell was as if a sweet summer air had swum over my agitated soul. It was the bell that announced the solemn moment when God became man, when the divine spirit, by the miracle of transubstantiation, became flesh and blood.

In an ecstasy of faith, of awe, I plunged on my face and adored and wept, and a mighty wind swept from the altar with strange moanings and lamentings, and the lights were extinguished; yet there was a luminous fog, that enfolded us, and in it I saw the great serpent, symbol of wisdom, symbol of eternity, rear spirally aloft, and beneath it — oh, beneath it! — was the Beatific Vision. In swelling nimbus of flame was a counterfeit Mother of God, and holding the hand of Him, of the Infant, Jesus, born but three hours, and — oh, the horror of it! — not *my* Christ, not *our* Christ, not the Christ of the Christians, but an Antichrist from some fetid hell, sent to seduce us, curse us, destroy us! My eyes almost burst from their sockets, and the humming of hell's loom roared about me as I met the gaze — of the Woman. And now her eyes were the serpent's eyes, and on her head was the crown of hell and its multiple kingdoms. She was naked, and set against her breasts were sharp swords. She was Mater Malorum, and her breath sowed discord, lust, and cruel murder. I yearned to pronounce the name of the true Mother of God, to bid this blinding vision, this

THE VISION MALEFIC

damnable vision, vanish, but my tongue was like wet twine and my sight blistered by the pageantry of Satan, of Satan and his Dam. And as I struggled the silvery little bell tapped once more, and in a fading perspective I saw the Madonna and the Child give me such a sweet, beseeching glance that my heart dissolved within me, and I cried aloud, my tongue snapping in the roof of my mouth:

"Mary, Mother of God, preserve us from the Devil and all his works!" A withering streak of light struck my eyeballs, and I glimpsed the serpent falling to earth with distended jaws, as two priestly figures reeled off the altar-steps, and in the brassy clangor of despair we fell, all three, and swooning blackness shut down upon us like smothering velvet.

It was still dark when solicitous hands lifted me to my feet: my coat was thrown about my shoulders, and I was hurried in shivering gloom to the street. The other one disappeared at the little postern gate, and, parting outside, with damp, hot hands, and face plastered with hideous passion, the mad priest said to me, in a cracked voice:

"You have seen *my* God, the only true God of hell — heaven and earth."

www.ingramcontent.com/pod-product-compliance
Lightning Source LLC
Chambersburg PA
CBHW060148050426
42446CB00013B/2729